the lesley stowe **fine foods cookbook**

the lesley stowe
fine foods cookbook

LESLEY STOWE

with a foreword from David Wood

HarperCollins*PublishersLtd*

The Lesley Stowe Fine Foods Cookbook
Recipes © 2006 by Lesley Stowe Fine Foods
Additional text © 2006 by Lesley Stowe and Jill Lambert
All rights reserved.

Published by HarperCollins Publishers Ltd

First Edition

No part of this book may be used or reproduced in any
manner whatsoever without the prior written permission
of the publisher, except in the case of brief quotations
embodied in reviews.

HarperCollins books may be purchased for educational,
business, or sales promotional use through our Special
Markets Department.

HarperCollins Publishers Ltd
2 Bloor Street East, 20th Floor
Toronto, Ontario, Canada
M4W 1A8

www.harpercollins.ca

Library and Archives Canada Cataloguing in Publication

Stowe, Lesley
The Lesley Stowe Fine Foods cookbook / Lesley
Stowe.—1st ed.

ISBN-13: 978-0-00-639584-3
ISBN-10: 0-00-639584-8

1. Cookery. I. Title.

TX714.S86 2006   641.5   C2006-902064-7

RRD 9 8 7 6 5 4 3 2 1

Printed and bound in the United States
Project Manager: Jill Lambert
Photography: Yvonne Duivenvoorden
Food Styling: Claire Stubbs
Prop Styling: Catherine Doherty

I dedicate this book to my husband, Geoffrey,
and stepchildren, Gillian and Douglas, with love.

Contents

Foreword

LESLEY STOWE ONCE TOLD ME that she made the decision to start her Fine Foods business after meeting and talking to me in the store I ran in Toronto. That I played a role in inspiring her to start her own business is a considerable compliment; but if I am honest it is also somewhat surprising. As far as I can remember, I was always extremely cautious about encouraging any one to take up specialty food retailing as a career. Some people may have thought that I simply wanted to discourage any competition; but I am, perhaps to my detriment, not that devious. I was simply telling the truth as I saw it – that fine food retailing is not an easy business.

Undeterred by whatever I may have said, Lesley went ahead and opened her store in Vancouver in the early '90s, and in doing so brought a new level of culinary awareness to the West Coast of Canada. When we opened our shop back in the '80s, good food was all about being international and cosmopolitan, and sophistication was defined by a person's knowledge of French cheeses, air dried European hams and how to tell the difference between Ossetra and Sevruga caviars. But things were beginning to change: a new style and approach to food was taking over. What we knew back then as California cuisine – using fresh and local produce in relatively simple preparations, in which sauces took a back seat to highlighting the essential flavours of the ingredients – was beginning to percolate northwards. In the past, Canadians

had found themselves travelling to find good food, but now the tables were turned; visitors were actually coming here to discover the foods that we grew and produced in our own backyard, and Lesley's shop was at the top of the list for gourmands seeking artisan products and creatively prepared local fare.

These last 15 years have been a very good time to be a small-scale food producer in British Columbia, and indeed throughout North America. It has also been a good time to be an afficionado of good food, because in that time there has been an explosion in the range and quality of locally available products, made possible by partnerships everywhere between growers and processors, chefs and retailers. Lesley's shop and adjoining catering company have been at the forefront of this transformation, she herself one of the leaders of the new wave.

From the perspective of a cookbook reader, a catering business is an excellent source of recipes. With catering there is an emphasis on variety, because the demand for culinary creativity ranges all the way from breakfast to late-night suppers. The ideas are interesting because clients are always looking for new and different ways to impress their guests. And as a home cook, you can be pretty confident that a caterer's recipes will work, for the simple reason that one experience of having to serve plates of something that "did not quite work out" to a roomful of discriminating guests

David Wood, Saltspring Island, B.C., 2006

is an experience that no one wants to repeat. Ever after, caterers make sure that all their dishes, even the new and interesting ones, have been tried and tested. Caterers' recipes combine variety, innovation and reliability, and, when you come right down to it, that is pretty much what you want out of a cookbook.

What is presented here is a collection of recipes by someone with a natural talent for cooking who has been instrumental in the business at a formative time for West Coast food and who continues to inspire chefs new and old throughout Vancouver and beyond. It is a book that captures the flavours of a place – and of the person who created them.

Introduction

IN 1990, I DECIDED TO BROADEN THE SCOPE OF MY CATERING COMPANY, Lesley Stowe Fine Foods, and enter the retail world. Up until this time, we were caterers with a reputation and image that was always based on the last event we catered. From the start, we had a reputation for fabulous desserts; we supplied several high-end restaurants in Vancouver and caused quite a stir with some of them. Our Death by Chocolate, which we created for Bishop's restaurant, got so much press that the restaurant eventually had to come up with their own version of it. (See page 168 for the original recipe.) Pierre Elliott Trudeau was known for ordering two servings of the dessert whenever he visited the restaurant. Needless to say, it developed quite a following.

I saw a real need for a store that offered more than the typical delis located throughout the city. My vision was to open a shop that offered fine food products from around the world, along with freshly prepared entrées, vegetables, salads and desserts from our own kitchen. The year I spent in Paris going to cooking school and eating my way through the city, I saw *traiteurs* (takeout shops) on almost every street corner doing this very thing (although even to this day pastry and bread command their own locations in France). I knew we could do it all here. A visit to David Wood Fine Food Store in Toronto confirmed my concept; his store was about the same size as the space we had secured and offered an array of packaged and fresh product. Our store was a new concept in Vancouver; I wanted to bring in fabulous extra-virgin olive oils, unpasteurized cheeses, specialty teas and coffee, but I also wanted to educate our customers on why they were better, what to look for in fine food and how to taste it. Sampling became an integral part of the experience at Lesley Stowe Fine Foods – learning through tasting.

My belief has always been that if you have the calling to be involved in the world of food, you carry with that a certain responsibility to educate and help people connect with food: where it comes from, how it is made or grown and how to support the existence of the handmade, organic and natural.

Until recently in North America, we have been caught up in the syndrome of more and faster is better. We are just starting to learn from smaller countries, where space and time are precious commodities, that we should nurture and appreciate the small independent farmer, grocer and restaurateur. With so much land available, farming in North America has been done on a massive scale, putting food production and manufacturing on an equally large scale. Fast food chains are an extension of that mentality.

When Lesley Stowe Fine Foods opened its doors in Vancouver, we were just beginning to see change on the West Coast. Granville Island Public Market had become a fixture and was changing the way people were shopping for produce, encouraging customers to pay attention to quality. This is what we were trying to do at Lesley Stowe Fine Foods. We were the first in the city to offer true artisanal bread, bringing in Manoucher loaves from Toronto and then seeking

out and offering space to a chef in Vancouver who wanted to bake slow-rise natural breads. So successful was this venture, he had to move out into his own space in the course of a year. We introduced Gelato Fresco, Valrhona chocolate from France, and when the threat to ban unpasteurized cheese from France loomed we had a lineup out the door to sign our petition. Luckily the voice of cheese lovers across the country was heard in Ottawa, and we are still able to enjoy some of those very special cheeses.

As a result of seeking out these amazing products and introducing Vancouver to them, I felt we needed to offer cooking and tasting classes. This allowed our customers the chance to cook in a commercial kitchen and actually use some of these products. Since that time we have seen a greater awareness of and demand for better selection and quality of food in the general marketplace, all the way up to the larger grocery stores that are offering organic and specialty sections. The population is growing, people are travelling more, and luckily Vancouver is rising to the occasion. Along with grocery stores filling the need, we are seeing the rise in independent farmers turning to heirloom varieties of produce and organic methods for production. Restaurants in a highly competitive arena are embracing this way of thinking.

My culinary philosophy is based on the influences around me, the training I have had and the passion I carry in spreading the theory, one that is coming forward everywhere in the culinary world to support sustainable ingredients and go back to our roots. It encourages people to spend more time in their kitchens and less time in their cars, to eat dinner as a family as opposed to reheating something quick in the microwave. Just think back to your first culinary memory: your grandmother's apple pie, real French onion soup in a Paris bistro, fresh oysters off the beach in PEI.

My own culinary epiphany came from a simple family restaurant in the little town of St. Marguerita, Italy. I don't think there was even a sign outside; certainly it hadn't been discovered by *Gourmet* or *Food & Wine* yet, as the place was packed with locals only. I ordered the pesto lasagna, which turned out to be totally unlike any lasagna I'd ever seen at home. It was thin sheets of flat pasta piled loosely on the plate and drizzled with bright green pesto, obviously freshly made that day, a splash of amazing olive oil and a sprinkle of fresh pepper. Heaven. It made me rethink all of my notions of Italian food and made me anxious to discover more and take that knowledge home. It was the start of a journey that I continue today.

My dreams and desires remain unchanged: to continually bring the best product possible to you and to encourage everyone to step back into the kitchen and invite family and friends to join you. Cooking should not be a chore; it should be an opportunity to share and connect.

I hope you find this book helps you with everyday meals, inspirational entertaining and getting your family involved. This is what Lesley Stowe Fine Foods is all about: sharing good food.

Chapter One

STARTERS

Hors d'oeuvres, appetizers, finger foods, nibbles and teasers all fall into this category: dishes that tantalize the taste buds and get your meal off to a great start. Or, in some cases, make up your entire meal – if you're dining tapas style.

My philosophy on starters (if you can call it that) is that they should set the tone for what follows but not upstage everything else. If you are having a sit-down dinner with lots of courses, it's probably best to keep the hors d'oeuvre offerings down to a dull roar, unless you are going to have drinks for more than an hour before sitting down at the table. I suggest some fabulous olives, perhaps something a little different such as Arbequina, niçoise, or Picholine olives to add some extra interest. Match these with a bowl of warm toasted almonds sprinkled with fleur de sel, and then maybe add one dip like the Sweet, Smoky and Spicy Red Pepper Dip and some Raincoast Crisps and flatbread.

If you are going to enjoy cocktails for longer than an hour, add one or two individual hors d'oeuvres to keep those with hearty appetites happy. If you are doing a full-on cocktail party, you want to allow 8 to 12 different items, with a mix of hot and cold hors d'oeuvres. And remember, it works best if you start with the cold hors d'oeuvres first and then move to the hot ones; guests rarely go back to cold once the hot ones appear unless it is a scorching summer day.

When it comes to starters that double as first courses – these and desserts are often my favourite parts of the meal because you can be more adventurous – I have always loved drama, texture and the combination of hot and cold. Two recipes that stand out for me are the Asparagus, Chèvre and Parmesan Phyllos, and the Beaujolais Figs with Prosciutto and Cambozola; both are delicious paired with salad greens for the first course of a dinner and give you the contrast of sweet, salty, hot with fresh, crispy, cold.

Remember to balance your party workload so you aren't in the kitchen all night. If your second course needs last-minute attention, serve something that is completely ready for the first course. Your guests are there to see you and you them, so you've got to emerge from the kitchen at some point and say hello!

Fire and Ice Salsa

Homemade salsa captures the texture and freshness of the ingredients better than most store-bought salsas do. This salsa is cooked, so you can make a batch or even a double batch and keep it handy in the fridge for two to three weeks. The fire and ice moniker comes from the contrast of the cool tomatoes and hit of heat from the cayenne and smoky paprika. Serve the salsa with tortilla chips, grilled chicken or fish.

Makes 3 1/2 cups (875 mL)

1/2 sweet red pepper, cored and seeded
1/4 cup (50 mL) sugar
1/3 cup (75 mL) diced yellow onion
1 large clove garlic, crushed
4 1/2 cups (1.125 L) canned roma tomatoes, drained and diced
2 tbsp (30 mL) balsamic vinegar
1 tsp (5 mL) cayenne pepper
1 tsp (5 mL) smoked paprika

Preheat the broiler or barbecue. Roast or grill the red pepper until the skin blackens and chars. Place in a bowl and let cool. Peel off the blackened skin and discard. Dice the pepper into small pieces.

In a small heavy saucepan over high heat, cook the sugar and 1 tbsp (15 mL) water until it starts to caramelize. Remove from heat when it reaches a mahogany colour, about 5 minutes.

Add the onion and garlic. Return to low heat and cook for 5 minutes. Add the tomatoes, vinegar, cayenne and paprika. Simmer, stirring occasionally, until thick, 20 to 30 minutes. Let cool. The salsa can be refrigerated for up to 3 weeks.

Sweet, Smoky and Spicy Red Pepper Dip

I love having this dip on hand as an all-purpose condiment. It adds a spicy kick to sandwiches and hamburgers. But don't stop there: try it spooned over steamed broccoli or dolloped onto grilled fish – that is, if you have any left over after serving it with pita crisps, sliced baguette, Grissini (page 64) or Original Raincoast Crisps.

Makes 1 1/2 cups (375 mL)

2 sweet red peppers
1 tbsp (15 mL) extra-virgin olive oil
1/4 yellow onion, thinly sliced
2 tsp (10 mL) minced jalapeño pepper
   (about 1 pepper, including some of the seeds for extra heat)
2 tsp (10 mL) ground cumin
1/4 tsp (1 mL) minced garlic
1/4 cup (50 mL) extra-virgin olive oil
1 tbsp (15 mL) blackstrap molasses
1 tbsp (15 mL) fresh lime juice
2 tbsp (30 mL) minced fresh parsley
Sea salt and freshly ground pepper

Preheat the broiler. Roast the whole red peppers under the broiler (or over an open flame on a gas stove) until the skin blackens and chars. Place in a bowl and let cool. Peel off the blackened skin and discard. Cut the peppers in half; remove the seeds and core.

In a small skillet, heat 1 tbsp (15 mL) oil over medium heat. Reduce heat slightly and cook the onion until translucent. Stir in the jalapeño pepper, cumin and garlic. Cook for 1 minute to release the fragrance. Remove from heat. Set aside and let cool.

In a food processor fitted with a steel blade, combine the peppers, onion mixture, 1/4 cup (50 mL) oil, molasses, lime juice, parsley, and salt and pepper to taste. Purée until a smooth paste forms. Taste and adjust the seasoning. The dip can be refrigerated for up to 1 week. Let come to room temperature before serving.

New Mexico Eggplant Pepita Dip

Most dips taste amazing because they're loaded with rich ingredients. Not this one – it's basically all vegetables, so it makes an ideal weekday snack. If you can entice your kids to eat it, you won't need to worry so much about veggies at dinner.

Makes 2 cups (500 mL)

1 sweet red pepper
1 large eggplant
1 tomato
1/4 cup (50 mL) pepitas (pumpkin seeds), shelled and roasted
1 clove garlic
2 tbsp (30 mL) minced fresh cilantro
1 tbsp (15 mL) fresh lime juice
1/4 tsp (1 mL) red pepper flakes
Sea salt and freshly ground pepper

Preheat the broiler. Roast the whole red pepper under the broiler (or over an open flame on a gas stove) until the skin blackens and chars. Place in a bowl and let cool. Peel off the blackened skin and discard. Cut the peppers in half; remove the seeds and core.

Preheat the oven to 350°F (180°C).

Prick the eggplant with a fork several times to help release the juices. Place on a baking sheet. Roast until very soft, about 1 hour. Let cool. Peel and discard the skin. In a food processor fitted with a steel blade, combine the roasted eggplant, roasted pepper, tomato, pepitas, garlic, cilantro, lime juice, red pepper flakes, and salt and pepper to taste. Purée until smooth. The dip can be refrigerated for up to 1 week.

Blue Cheese and Caramelized Onion Dip

In this luscious, rich dip, the saltiness of the blue cheese contrasts with the sweetness of the caramelized onions. It's fabulous with Raincoast Crisps – try the Cranberry Hazelnut or Rosemary Raisin versions.

Makes 2 cups (500 mL)

1 tbsp (15 mL) olive oil
1/4 onion, thinly sliced
3/4 cup (175 mL) sour cream
1/4 cup (50 mL) mayonnaise
6 oz (180 g) cream cheese
3 oz (90 g) blue cheese (Roquefort, Danish blue or Stilton)
4 tsp (20 mL) fresh lemon juice
Sea salt and freshly ground pepper

In a small sauté pan, heat the oil over medium-low heat; cook the onion, covered and stirring occasionally, until deep golden brown, about 20 minutes. Let cool.

In a bowl, whisk together the sour cream and mayonnaise. Add the cream cheese and blue cheese and mash with a rubber spatula until smooth. Stir in the caramelized onions and lemon juice. Season to taste with salt and pepper. Refrigerate until ready to serve.

Basil and Baby Shrimp Dip

The basil and shrimp marry well because the slight licorice overtone of the herb complements the delicate flavour of the shellfish. Be sure your shrimp is superfresh. If you can, smell it before you buy it; it should smell fresh, like ocean air. Also, try to add the basil as soon as you chop it; it oxidizes quickly and turns brown when the leaves are cut. You want to get the flavour into the dip, not leave it on the cutting board. This recipe is easily adapted: try substituting fresh dill for the basil and yogurt for the sour cream; if opting for the latter, use thick yogurt (I like Liberty brand).

Makes 3 cups (750 mL)

3/4 cup (175 mL) sour cream
3/4 cup (175 mL) mayonnaise
1 lb (500 g) fresh-cooked hand-peeled baby shrimp
   (see Cocktail Shrimp, below)
3 green onions, finely chopped
2 tbsp (30 mL) finely chopped fresh basil
1 tsp (5 mL) Tabasco sauce
1 tsp (5 mL) Worcestershire sauce
1 tsp (5 mL) grated lemon zest
Sea salt and freshly ground pepper

In a bowl, stir together the sour cream and mayonnaise. Mix in the shrimp, onions, basil, Tabasco and Worcestershire sauces, and lemon zest. Season to taste with salt and pepper. Cover and refrigerate until serving. The dip can be refrigerated for up to 2 days.

Cocktail Shrimp In Central and Eastern Canada, tiny cooked shrimp is often called "cocktail" shrimp; it's used for shrimp cocktail and shrimp sandwiches. On the West Coast, we refer to this shrimp as either hand-peeled or machine-peeled shrimp, depending on how the shells have come off. It's always sold cooked, and there's no need to devein it. No matter what you call it, please use the fresh variety, not the canned or frozen versions, for the recipes in this book. You're looking for baby shrimp about the size of a nickel, pale pink in colour with firm texture. It shouldn't have any smell other than salt air. Because it goes off very quickly, try to buy it the day you plan to use it or, at the most, the day before.

Muffuletta

One of the most versatile condiments you'll ever find, muffuletta originated in New Orleans, where it's used as a sandwich filling. Bursting with flavour, it makes an interesting addition to soup, tomato sauce, pizza and pasta. Double the batch and give some to a friend. It's a staple in my fridge; I serve it on Original Raincoast Crisps or baguette slices, either straight up or partnered with David Wood's soft goat cheese.

Makes 2 cups (500 mL)

3/4 cup (175 mL) green olives stuffed with pimento
1/4 cup (50 mL) kalamata olives, pitted
1/4 cup (50 mL) artichoke hearts
1/4 cup (50 mL) sun-dried tomatoes, softened
1/8 red onion
1 tbsp (15 mL) capers, drained
2 cloves garlic
2 anchovy fillets
1/4 cup (50 mL) olive oil
1/4 tsp (1 mL) sambal oelek*
1 tsp (5 mL) balsamic vinegar
1 tbsp (15 mL) chopped fresh rosemary
1 tbsp (15 mL) chopped fresh parsley
1/4 tsp (1 mL) dried oregano
1/4 tsp (1 mL) freshly ground pepper
Sea salt and freshly ground pepper

Finely chop the green and kalamata olives, artichokes, sun-dried tomatoes, onion, capers, garlic and anchovies. Place in a bowl and stir to combine. Add oil, sambal oelek, vinegar, rosemary, parsley, oregano and pepper; stir again. Season to taste with salt and pepper.

* Sambal oelek is an Indonesian-style spicy sauce made from chilies, salt and vinegar. Look for it in the Asian food section of supermarkets. If you can't find it, substitute chili sauce.

Olive and Fig Tapenade

This is a bit of a twist on traditional tapenade. The figs add sweetness and soften the salty bite of the olive. They also provide an interesting texture. Serve this with toasted baguette rounds. It makes an interesting pizza topping, or try it as a filling in a quesadilla with chicken and Camembert. The tapenade is best made a day in advance so the flavours can mellow.

Makes 1 3/4 cups (425 mL)

1 cup (250 mL) Mission figs, quartered
1 cup (250 mL) pitted niçoise olives or other brined black olives
1 tbsp (15 mL) capers, drained
1 large clove garlic, crushed
1 tsp (5 mL) fresh thyme leaves
3 tbsp (45 mL) olive oil
1 tbsp (15 mL) fresh lemon juice
Sea salt and freshly ground pepper

In a food processor, roughly chop the figs. Add the olives, capers, garlic and thyme; pulse until combined and slightly coarse. Add the oil and lemon juice; pulse to combine. Season to taste with salt and pepper. Cover and refrigerate until ready to serve. The tapenade can be refrigerated for up to 3 weeks.

Parmesan Crisps

This was the first crisp LSFF ever made. We sell these in our signature boutique only, as production costs don't allow us to wholesale them. Now you can try making a batch on your own. There are two keys to the success of this recipe, and both concern the baguette: look for the best quality available, and consider the crumb. It's important to use a ficelle or baguette with a dense crumb; otherwise, when you bake it, it will crumble easily. You have to let the baguette dry out overnight because you'll never be able to slice a fresh baguette thinly enough. Parmesan and pecorino are the best cheeses for this recipe as they are quite dry, thus keeping the final product dry and crisp as well.

Makes about 60 pieces

1/4 cup (50 mL) olive oil
3 cloves garlic, halved lengthwise
1 day-old ficelle or baguette
2 cups (500 mL) grated Parmesan cheese

In a small saucepan, combine the oil and garlic over medium-high heat. Slowly bring to a boil. Remove from heat and let cool for 30 minutes.

Preheat the oven to 250°F (120°C).

Slice the ficelle on a 45-degree angle as thinly as possible. Line a baking sheet with parchment paper and lay the bread slices in a single layer on the paper. Brush each slice with the garlic-infused oil and sprinkle evenly with the cheese. Bake until crisp and slightly golden, 15 to 20 minutes. The crisps can be stored in an airtight container for up to 2 weeks.

Onion Confit on Challah Toasts

Challah is an egg bread that's very soft and has a fine crumb. You can substitute brioche, or if you can't find either, use a baguette. When challah is toasted, the contrast between the crisp exterior and soft interior is part of the pleasure. A baguette will work nicely, too, although the texture will be chewier. The confit can be made in advance and refrigerated for up to one week. I like to make extra so I have it on hand to pair with a steak or slide into a sandwich with tomatoes and chèvre.

Makes 2 dozen pieces

6 thick slices (1 inch/2.5 cm) challah or brioche

Onion Confit:
3 tbsp (45 mL) olive oil
2 tbsp (30 mL) unsalted butter
2 sweet onions, halved lengthwise, then thinly sliced lengthwise into strips
1 tbsp (15 mL) packed brown sugar
1/3 cup (75 mL) red wine
1 tbsp (15 mL) balsamic vinegar
Coarse sea salt and freshly ground pepper

Onion Confit: In a heavy skillet, heat the oil and butter over low heat; cook the onions until softened but not browned, about 20 minutes. Sprinkle with the brown sugar and continue cooking over low heat until evenly browned. Stir in the wine and vinegar and simmer until the liquid is completely absorbed. Season to taste with salt and pepper. Set aside.

Preheat the broiler. Arrange the challah slices on a baking sheet and toast under the broiler until just barely golden, 1 to 2 minutes. Turn over and toast for 1 to 2 minutes longer. Transfer to a rack and let cool. Cut off the crusts and slice each into 4 triangles. Top each triangle with a spoonful of Onion Confit to serve.

Shrimp Bruschetta with Red Pepper Aïoli

In Italy, bruschetta has always been a great way to use up bread that isn't totally fresh, and to this day it remains fairly simple – slices of bread grilled, rubbed with garlic and brushed with olive oil. When tomatoes are in season, chopped tomato and basil top this creation.

In North America, we always like to add a twist; this recipe takes some liberties, but I think you'll agree the results are worth it.

Makes 2 dozen

1 tsp (5 mL) olive oil
1 large clove garlic, minced
1/2 tsp (2 mL) red pepper flakes
3/4 lb (375 g) fresh-cooked hand-peeled baby shrimp
2 tbsp (30 mL) capers, drained
12 thick (1/2-inch) slices fresh bread
   (sourdough, French or other artisan variety)
Red Pepper Aïoli (recipe follows)

In a small saucepan, heat the oil over medium-low heat; cook the garlic and red pepper flakes until garlic starts to sizzle, but do not allow it to brown. Remove from heat and immediately add the shrimp and capers. Mix well and set aside.

Preheat the broiler. Cut two 2-inch (5 cm) triangles out of each bread slice. Place on a baking sheet and toast under the broiler until light brown, about 1 minute. Turn over and toast for 1 minute longer.

Spoon some of the shrimp mixture on top of each triangle and top with a small dollop of Red Pepper Aïoli. Serve immediately.

Aïoli is a very garlicky mayonnaise that originated in Provence, in the south of France. The word comes from ail, meaning garlic, and oli, meaning oil. Aïoli is made from garlic, egg yolks, lemon juice and olive oil. It's a gutsy, fragrant sauce to serve with chicken, fish or vegetables.

The classic garlic mayonnaise so popular in France is livened up here with roasted red pepper, which adds sweet flavour and a beautiful colour. The sambal oelek provides a bit of spicy flavour and colour, too.

Red Pepper Aïoli

1 sweet red pepper
1/2 cup (125 mL) mayonnaise
1/2 tsp (2 mL) very finely minced garlic
1/4 tsp (1 mL) sambal oelek or chili sauce

Preheat the broiler. Place the whole red pepper on a baking sheet and broil until the skin blackens and chars. Place in a bowl and let cool. Peel off the blackened skin and discard. Cut the pepper in half; remove the seeds and core.

In a food processor, combine the roasted pepper, mayonnaise, garlic and sambal oelek. Blend until smooth.

Smoked Salmon and Avocado Tartare on Crispy Won Tons

These were inspired by a dish I enjoyed at a restaurant in Portland, Oregon. They look as good as they taste. The combination of the pink salmon and the pale green avocado is delicate and fresh, the flavour rich and luscious. Making the crispy won tons is actually really easy, but in a pinch, you can use a good-quality tortilla chip. To save time, make the won tons a few days in advance; store in an airtight container. The avocado mixture is best served immediately, but you can refrigerate it overnight, placing plastic wrap directly on the surface to prevent browning.

Makes 36 pieces, 8 generous servings

2 cups (500 mL) peanut or grape seed oil
18 won ton wrappers, cut in half diagonally
3 ripe avocados
1 tbsp (15 mL) fresh lime juice
1/2 tsp (2 mL) sea salt
1 jalapeño, minced (including some of the seeds for extra heat if you like)
1 tsp (5 mL) minced garlic
1 large roma tomato, seeded and finely diced
18 slices cold smoked salmon, cut in half
6 tbsp (90 mL) crème fraîche (page 25)
Fresh cilantro leaves
Freshly ground pepper

In a heavy, straight-sided skillet, heat oil to 250°F (120°C), just before it reaches the smoking point; deep-fry the won ton wrappers until golden, about 30 seconds. Drain on paper towels and let cool.

Finely dice 1 1/2 of the avocados and mash the rest in a bowl. Stir together the mashed avocado, lime juice, salt, jalapeño pepper and garlic. Fold in the tomato and diced avocado.

Drop a small spoonful of the avocado mixture in the centre of each won ton. Drape a piece of smoked salmon on top. Garnish each with about 1/4 tsp (1 mL) of the crème fraîche, a cilantro leaf and a grinding of pepper.

Sea Salt

Essential to great cooking, salt is a basic ingredient that should never be taken for granted. Properly used, the right kind of salt brings out the best in food and can make all the difference between a dish that's just okay and one that's very good.

The most commonly available variety is table salt. It's been iodized, which tends to give it a bitter flavour; phosphates or starch are added to keep the salt free of clumps, so it pours freely.

Replacing table salt with sea salt is a simple way to improve your culinary experience. Because it's full of minerals, it has a much more interesting flavour. Sea salt comes in coarse or fine grind or in flakes. It's easy to find, and most brands are reasonably priced. For all the recipes in this book, I recommend using sea salt. It's actually my secret mission to rid all the kitchens I visit of table salt and relegate it to the garage, ready for melting snow off the driveway.

The ultimate sea salt is fleur de sel, which comes from the Guérande region on the west coast of France. Because it's hand-harvested, it's still slightly damp when you take it out of the jar. Although fleur de sel is expensive, it's exquisite as a condiment or finishing salt. If you have the opportunity to buy some, give yourself a treat – it's worth the price. The best way to use it is as a garnish on sliced vine-ripened tomatoes, on roasted potatoes hot out of the oven, or on a steak straight from the grill.

Salt has become such a darling of the culinary world in the past few years that all sorts of exotic varieties are now available. In red sea salt from Hawaii, volcanic clay is actually added to give it colour. Or try black sea salt, which has a strong sulphuric taste that works well in Indian cooking. C Restaurant in Vancouver smokes sea salt and packages it for retail sale across the country. A pinch of it on grilled tuna or salmon is sublime.

Mediterranean Torta

This takes a bit of effort to make, but the results are truly worthwhile. Make the Sun-Dried Tomato Pesto a day or two in advance and refrigerate, covered, until you're ready to complete the dish. Or if you're really strapped for time, you can use a high-quality purchased pesto rather than make your own.

Makes 8 servings

1 lb (500 g) cream cheese, softened
3/4 lb (375 g) soft chèvre
1/2 cup (125 mL) Sun-Dried Tomato Pesto (recipe follows)
1/2 cup (125 mL) Basil Pesto (recipe follows)
Fresh basil leaves
Pine nuts or sun-dried tomatoes

Line the bottom of a 7-inch (1.5 L) springform pan with parchment paper or waxed paper. Blend together the cream cheese and chèvre until smooth. Spread a layer of the cheese mixture (1/3 of the total amount) on the paper. Top with the Sun-dried Tomato Pesto, then carefully top with another layer of the cheese mixture. Spread with the Basil Pesto, then top with more of the cheese mixture.

The torta can be covered and refrigerated until serving, or it can be wrapped and frozen. To serve, run a hot knife around the edge of the pan and remove the ring. Run a spatula under the torta to separate it from the parchment paper and carefully slide it onto a plate. Decorate with basil leaves and pine nuts or sun-dried tomatoes. Serve with Raincoast Crisps or thin baguette slices.

Sun-Dried Tomato Pesto

Makes 2 cups (500 mL)

2 cups (500 mL) oil-packed sun-dried tomatoes, drained
5 cloves garlic
2/3 cup (150 mL) grated Parmesan cheese

Drain the oil from the tomatoes and reserve. You'll need about 3/4 cup (175 mL) of oil; top up with olive oil if necessary.

In a food processor, blend together tomatoes, garlic and cheese until smooth. Add the oil gradually, processing until the pesto reaches an ideal spreading consistency.

If you're substituting dry-packed tomatoes, cover them with boiling water and let stand for 10 to 15 minutes before using; drain. Then substitute olive oil for the reserved oil called for in the recipe.

Basil Pesto

Makes 3/4 cup (175 mL)

1 cup (250 mL) fresh basil leaves, washed and stemmed
3/4 cup (175 mL) fresh parsley, washed and stemmed
2 cloves garlic
1 tbsp (15 mL) pine nuts
1/2 tsp (2 mL) freshly ground pepper
1/2 cup (125 mL) grated Parmesan cheese
1/3 cup (75 mL) olive oil

In a food processor, combine the basil, parsley, garlic, pine nuts and pepper; blend until smooth. Add the cheese and blend again. Pour in the oil and process just until incorporated.

Basil Pesto is a classic condiment that enhances pasta dishes, soups and even mashed potatoes. A handy way to store individual portions is to fill an ice cube tray with pesto and freeze it. Once frozen, pop out the cubes and store them in a freezer bag. Or you can line a baking sheet with plastic wrap, drop spoonfuls of pesto onto the wrap and then freeze. When frozen, transfer them to a resealable freezer bag to use as needed.

Onigiri with Teriyaki Aïoli

Onigiri are Japanese rice cakes flavoured with chili sauce, vegetables and herbs. They're crispy on the outside and chewy on the inside. Children love them; however, you might want to leave out the chili sauce to suit them. Get your kids to help form the rice into various shapes – the traditional version is a triangle.

Kejap manis is Indonesian sweet soy sauce. Look for it in the Asian section of large grocery stores. If you can't find it, substitute equal parts soy sauce and brown sugar, simmered until sugar is dissolved.

Makes 6 servings, about 24 onigiri

2 tbsp (30 mL) olive oil
2 tsp (10 mL) minced garlic
1/2 large onion, minced
3/4 cup (175 mL) minced celery
2 cups (500 mL) well-rinsed Japanese sushi rice (available in the Asian section of many supermarkets)
2 1/2 cups (625 mL) water
2 tbsp (30 mL) kejap manis*
2 tbsp (30 mL) sambal oelek or chili paste
1 small sweet red pepper, minced
1 1/2 bunches fresh cilantro, minced
1/4 cup (50 mL) sesame oil
Teriyaki Aïoli (recipe follows)

In a saucepan, heat the oil over medium heat; sauté the garlic, onion and celery until softened. Stir in the rice, water, kejap manis, sambal oelek and red pepper. Cover and bring to a boil over medium-high heat. Reduce heat and simmer until the water is absorbed, 15 to 20 minutes. Remove from heat and let stand, covered, for 10 minutes. When cool, mix in the cilantro. With wet hands, form about 1/4 cup (50 mL) of the rice mixture into a triangular shape. Squeeze together tightly to form solid cake. Repeat with remaining rice mixture. Refrigerate, uncovered, for at least 2 hours or for up to 24 hours to allow the onigiri to set up and stay firm.

Brush the onigiri with sesame oil. Place on a greased grill or in a grill pan over medium heat and cook, turning once, until crispy and light brown, about 2 minutes per side. Onigiri can be made in advance and reheated in the oven. Serve warm with the Teriyaki Aïoli for dipping.

Aïoli is mayonnaise flavoured with garlic. This version is quite spicy, with Asian flavours of sesame, ginger and soy. Leftovers will last about a week; use it on chicken, fish – even a tuna sandwich – or as a dip for veggies.

Teriyaki Aïoli

Makes 2 1/2 cups (625 mL)

3 tbsp (45 mL) sesame seeds
2 eggs
2 tbsp (30 mL) fresh lemon juice
2 cloves garlic
3/4 tsp (4 mL) sea salt
1/4 tsp (1 mL) mustard (grainy, Dijon or dry)
1 cup (250 mL) olive oil
1 cup (250 mL) vegetable oil
1/4 cup (50 mL) liquid honey
1/4 cup (50 mL) minced green onions
3 tbsp (45 mL) soy sauce
3 tbsp (45 mL) minced fresh cilantro
2 tbsp (30 mL) ginger juice*
2 tbsp (30 mL) minced fresh gingerroot

*Ginger juice is obtained by placing freshly grated gingerroot in a damp cheesecloth or clean J cloth and squeezing out the juice. Two inches (5 cm) of gingerroot yields about 2 tbsp (30 mL) juice.

In a dry skillet over medium heat, toast the sesame seeds until golden brown. Remove from heat and set aside to cool.

In a food processor, blend together the eggs, lemon juice, garlic, salt and mustard. Whisk together the olive and vegetable oils. Adding drop by drop through the feed tube, pulse in enough of the oil until mixture thickens and emulsifies. Add the remaining oil in a steady stream. Mix in the toasted sesame seeds, honey, onions, soy sauce, cilantro, ginger juice and gingerroot until combined.

Asparagus, Chèvre and Parmesan Phyllos

This has been a favourite hors d'oeuvre since it first hit the cocktail party circuit. The combination of melted chèvre, asparagus and crispy phyllo is a slightly decadent teaser. I often add a bit of prosciutto for another layer of flavour.

Makes 24 pieces

6 sheets phyllo pastry
2/3 cup (150 mL) melted butter
2/3 cup (150 mL) grated Parmesan cheese
8 raw asparagus spears
6 oz (180 g) soft chèvre
1 green onion, chopped

Preheat the oven to 375°F (190°C).

Place 1 sheet of the phyllo pastry on work surface. Brush with some of the butter and sprinkle with some of the Parmesan. Top with another sheet; brush with more butter and sprinkle with more Parmesan. Top with third sheet and brush with more butter. Cut the phyllo stack in half lengthwise. Repeat with the remaining 3 phyllo sheets, reserving some of the Parmesan.

Lay the asparagus spears along the long edge of each phyllo stack. Dot with some of the chèvre and sprinkle with green onion. Roll up. Brush with butter and sprinkle with the remaining Parmesan.

Place, seam side down, on a baking sheet and bake until golden. Cut each roll crosswise into 6 pieces.

Better Butter

Butter plays a huge role in cooking and baking and, as with so many other key ingredients, the better the quality the better the taste of the final product. I use only unsalted butter, which is usually made with cream that's fresher than the cream in salted butter. Salt acts as a preservative, so the cream lasts longer, but that's not always a good thing because it covers up the freshness. Using unsalted butter also gives you control over the amount of salt in the finished dish.

Sometimes you will come across European-style butter, which has a higher butterfat content and is made by churning the cream more slowly, for longer, giving it a creamier taste and silkier texture.

If you have the opportunity to visit France, you will see that the array of butter in the local markets for sale is amazing. Like cheeses from different regions, butter tastes different from one area to the next depending on what the cows eat and their environment.

Beaujolais Figs with Prosciutto and Cambozola

This is a brilliant little treat, combining the qualities of sweet and salty. The bonus is that it's so easy to make. When fresh figs are in season, it gets even easier: simply quarter the figs, place a piece of Cambozola on each piece and wrap with prosciutto for an instant hors d'oeuvre.

Makes 40 pieces

10 dried figs, preferably Calimyrna or Mission
1 1/2 cups (375 mL) Beaujolais or dry red wine
1 wedge (2 inches/5 cm) Cambozola, torn into small pieces
10 slices prosciutto, each cut into 4 strips (1 per fig quarter)

Preheat the oven to 300°F (150°C).

In a saucepan over medium-low heat, combine whole figs and wine. Poach the figs in the wine until softened, about 20 minutes. Drain, discarding the wine. Quarter the figs lengthwise. Place a piece of Cambozola on each fig quarter and wrap in a prosciutto strip. Place on a baking sheet and bake just until cheese starts to melt, 3 to 4 minutes.

Fish and Chips

A play on words, this tasty hors d'oeuvre is a good pre-dinner drinks teaser – it will get your palate ready for the main event without filling you up. It's just a thin slice of potato baked until crispy and topped with crème fraîche, chives and caviar.

Makes 20 pieces

1/3 cup (75 mL) crème fraîche (page 25)
1 tsp (5 mL) finely grated lemon zest
1/2 tsp (2 mL) minced chives
Sea salt
2 tbsp (30 mL) olive oil
2 large russet potatoes, peeled
3 oz (90 g) caviar, preferably osetra or lumpfish

SPECIAL EQUIPMENT
Mandoline or other manual slicer (the little Japanese ones are good)
1 1/2- to 2-inch (3.5 to 5 cm) star-shaped cookie cutter

Preheat the oven to 375°F (190°C).

Stir together the crème fraîche, lemon zest and chives. Season to taste with salt. Refrigerate until ready to use.

Brush 2 large baking sheets with oil. Using a mandoline, slice the potatoes crosswise on a slight diagonal, about 1/8 inch (3 mm) thick. Using a cookie cutter, cut out star shapes from potato slices; arrange in a single layer on baking sheets. Brush stars with more oil and season with salt.

Bake the potato stars, in batches, in the middle of the oven until golden and crisp, about 15 minutes. (Some of the stars may curl up a bit.) Using a metal spatula, carefully transfer to paper towels to drain and crisp. Let cool for 2 minutes. Top each star with a dollop of the crème fraîche mixture and a sprinkling of caviar.

Spicy Smoked Salmon Corn Cakes with Crème Fraîche

Smoked salmon is a familiar treat on the West Coast, and we're always looking for new ways to serve it. Here, the corn cake itself is neutral, creating a perfect vehicle for the smoked salmon, corn and jalapeño peppers. Serve this on organic greens with a citrus vinaigrette for an interesting starter. If you'd prefer it as an hors d'oeuvre, simply make the corn cakes smaller, about the size of a toonie.

Makes 8 servings

3/4 cup (175 mL) yellow cornmeal
6 tbsp (90 mL) all-purpose flour
1/2 tsp (2 mL) baking soda
1/2 tsp (2 mL) sea salt
2 large eggs, lightly beaten
3/4 cup (125 mL) buttermilk
6 tbsp (90 mL) cream cheese, at room temperature
1 cup (250 mL) frozen corn kernels
4 tbsp (60 mL) minced chives
4 jalapeño peppers, seeded and minced
4 oz (125 g) smoked salmon, minced (about 1/3 cup/75 mL)
4 tbsp (60 mL) vegetable oil
Crème fraîche, chopped red onion and lemon slices

In a small bowl, whisk together the cornmeal, flour, baking soda and salt. In another bowl, whisk together the eggs, buttermilk and cream cheese. Chop half of the corn coarsely and stir into the buttermilk mixture along with remaining corn, chives, jalapeños and salmon. Fold into the cornmeal mixture, stirring just until combined.

In a large non-stick skillet, heat the oil over medium-high heat until hot but not smoking. In batches, drop batter by 2 tbsp (30 mL) measures into the skillet and spread slightly to form 3- to 4-inch (8.5 to 10 cm) cakes. Cook until golden brown, 2 to 3 minutes per side. Transfer to a heatproof platter and keep warm. Serve with crème fraîche, chopped red onion and lemon slices.

This recipe is so versatile we could have placed it in any section of this book – it shows up everywhere. A staple in French kitchens, this thick, rich, slightly tart cream is fabulous as an accompaniment to many foods. It goes well with seafood, as its delicate flavour doesn't overwhelm. It's also wonderful with desserts, especially with caramel and chocolate. Ready-made crème fraîche is often hard to find in stores, but it's easy to make – it just takes a little planning.

Crème Fraîche

Makes 1 cup (250 mL)

1 cup (250 mL) heavy cream (try not to buy ultra-pasteurized)
1 tbsp (15 mL) buttermilk or natural organic plain yogurt

In a saucepan over very low heat, combine the heavy cream and buttermilk; warm, stirring constantly, just until it reaches body temperature. Pour into a metal or glass bowl; cover with plastic and place in a warm spot in your kitchen. Let thicken for 24 to 48 hours. It should look like yogurt or sour cream. Refrigerate until ready to use (it will thicken further in the fridge).

Chapter Two
SOUPS & SALADS

Elegant soups with seafood, vegetable soups and classic chicken soup with a twist – soup is a great beginning, or a meal in itself. Follow it up with salad – special greens with cheese and fruit – and some gutsy artisan bread.

At LSFF, our daily soups have a real following. There's nothing quite like homemade soup for lunch on a damp, wet day. Or as an elegant start to a dinner party, try the Vichyssoise with Dungeness Crab and Frizzled Leeks. Soups can be the star or just a teaser, and they're a perfect canvas for your imagination. Once you have a good stock for the base, there's no limit to the soup creations you can invent.

Salads are a creative category in their own right. At LSFF, we are always on the hunt for interesting ideas for salads as a perfect match to the entrées we sell. More traditional salads were soon paired with new dressings and delicious combinations of cheese and fruit. We also offer lots of grilled salads, from potatoes to asparagus, all adding a new dimension to the traditional vision of what a salad can be.

With all the farmers' markets that have sprung up across the country, we now have access to an incredible array of micro-greens, from mustard greens and mizuna to arugula and baby spinach – either mixed together or, as is my preference, served on their own. I encourage you to use your imagination and, depending on your taste preferences, add toasted nuts (toasting brings out the full flavour), cheese, dried or fresh fruit and a spectacular vinaigrette. The only rule I recommend is to not mix too many different flavours. You want the individual flavours to stand out.

Kathy's Chicken Soup

Kathy used to work in the kitchen at LSFF, where she created this homey and comforting soup. This is my husband Geoffrey's favourite chicken soup – no substitutes need apply. The dried mixture known as herbes de Provence – thyme, rosemary, savory, oregano and marjoram – gives this soup its distinctive flavour. You can find herbes de Provence in most grocery stores.

Makes 3 quarts (3 L)

1 whole chicken (2 to 3 lb/1 to 1.5 kg)
3 quarts (3 L) cold chicken stock
1 tbsp (15 mL) herbes de Provence
3/4 cup (175 mL) finely chopped carrots
3/4 cup (175 mL) finely diced new potatoes
3/4 cup (175 mL) fresh or frozen corn niblets
3/4 cup (175 mL) fresh or frozen peas
1/2 cup (125 mL) finely chopped sweet red pepper
Sea salt and freshly ground pepper

In a large stockpot, cover the chicken with stock and bring to a boil. Reduce heat and simmer for 1 hour. Reserving the liquid, transfer the chicken to a bowl and let cool. Skim the fat from the surface and strain the solids from the stock. Return the strained stock to the stockpot; add the herbes de Provence, carrots and potatoes and simmer until just barely tender. Add the corn, peas and red pepper. Heat through until vegetables are tender-crisp, about 5 minutes.

Meanwhile, remove the meat from the chicken carcass by cutting the breast along the bone. Slide your fingers underneath the breast meat and pull it off the bone. Detach each leg and pull the meat off the bone. Cut the chicken meat into 1/2-inch (1 cm) pieces and add to the simmering soup; heat through for 5 minutes. To serve, season to taste with salt and pepper.

Pappardelle Tomato Cannellini Bean Soup

If you've spent time in Italy, you'll appreciate how Italians can take the simplest ingredients and elevate them to another level. This very easy dish is true comfort food. It does take a little time to prepare – the beans have to soak overnight – but the results are worth the effort. Pappardelle are wide ribbon noodles. They're cooked separately to avoid overcooking. If you can't find pappardelle, use fettuccine or skip the pasta altogether. This makes a great healthy dinner. Serve it with a loaf of olive bread.

Makes 3 quarts (3 L)

1/2 lb (250 g) cannellini beans, washed and picked over
3 tbsp (45 mL) olive oil
1 1/2 oz (45 g) lean pancetta, chopped (1/4 cup/50 mL packed)
1 clove garlic, minced
1 stalk celery, chopped
1 cup (250 mL) chopped fennel
1 large onion, chopped
1 carrot, chopped
1 tsp (5 mL) sea salt
1/4 tsp (1 mL) red pepper flakes
1/2 cup (125 mL) chopped canned Italian plum tomatoes
1 small sprig fresh rosemary (or 1/4 tsp/1 mL dried)
1 lb (500 g) pappardelle
1 tsp (5 mL) fresh gingerroot, minced
3 to 4 tbsp (45 to 60 mL) extra-virgin olive oil
1/2 cup (125 mL) grated Parmesan cheese

In a large pot, cover the beans with water and soak overnight. Drain.

In a large heavy stockpot, heat 3 tbsp (45 mL) of the oil over medium heat; sauté the pancetta until it begins to brown, 5 to 10 minutes. Add the garlic and sauté for 3 to 5 minutes. Add the celery, fennel, onion, carrot, salt and red pepper flakes. Reduce heat to low and sauté until softened, about 10 minutes.

Add the drained beans to the stockpot along with 8 cups (2 L) water, the tomatoes and rosemary; bring to a boil. Reduce heat and simmer until the beans are soft but not mushy, 1 to 1 1/2 hours. Remove from heat and let cool.

In a large pot, bring 5 quarts (5 L) salted water to a boil. Cook the pappardelle until al dente. Drain.

Meanwhile, transfer 3 cups (750 mL) of the soup to a food processor and purée it with the gingerroot; return the purée to the stockpot. This will thicken the soup and give it a silky texture. Bring to a simmer.

Ladle the soup into heated soup bowls. Divide the pappardelle among the bowls. Drizzle with the extra-virgin olive oil and sprinkle with cheese. Serve immediately.

Winter Tomato Soup with Orange and Ginger

Tomatoes are at their best straight from the field or your garden, still warm, packed with flavour and juice that pours down your chin when you bite into that first tomato sandwich of summer. For the rest of the year, we have to find a substitute. Unlike other varieties, Italian plum tomatoes are canned in season, capturing that flavour with less water and more flesh. Try to use the San Marzano variety if you can find it.

Makes 1 quart (1 L)

1 can (28 oz/796 mL) Italian plum tomatoes
1/2 cup (125 mL) freshly squeezed orange juice
1 tsp (5 mL) grated fresh gingerroot
Sea salt and freshly ground pepper
Yogurt (optional)

Strain the seeds from the tomatoes by pressing the pulp through a fine sieve. In a blender, combine the tomato pulp, orange juice and gingerroot; blend until smooth. Add salt and pepper to taste. Serve hot, or let cool then refrigerate to serve chilled. Garnish with a spoonful of yogurt, if desired.

Summer Gazpacho with Warm Focaccia Croutons

This is a summer soup because it's best with field-ripened tomatoes. Hothouse tomatoes really won't cut it here. Add water if necessary to thin the soup a bit; it should have a bit of body but not be stodgy. Since the flavouring can go flat when it's ice cold, check the seasoning after it's been chilled.

Makes 6 servings

10 vine-ripened tomatoes
1 English cucumber, peeled
1 sweet red pepper
1 red onion
2 large cloves garlic, crushed
2 tbsp (30 mL) red wine vinegar
1/2 cup (125 mL) water
1 tsp (5 mL) sea salt
1/4 tsp (1 mL) freshly ground pepper

Focaccia Croutons:
1 square (6 inches/15 cm) focaccia, cut into 1/4-inch (5 mm) cubes
1 tbsp (15 mL) olive oil
1/2 English cucumber, finely diced
1 tbsp (15 mL) finely chopped chives

Quarter the tomatoes and place in a large bowl. Cut the cucumber, red pepper and red onion into 1-inch (2.5 cm) chunks. Add to the bowl along with the garlic; stir to combine. In a food processor, blend the vegetables in batches until smooth. There will be bits of pepper and tomato skins floating around but don't worry. Strain the purée through a sieve to remove the skins and seeds, pressing all the liquid and purée through. Stir in the vinegar, water, salt and pepper. Refrigerate the gazpacho until chilled. The gazpacho can be covered and refrigerated for up to 2 days, ready to serve.

Focaccia Croutons: Just before serving, toast the focaccia cubes in a dry sauté pan over medium-high heat, tossing, until golden brown. Drizzle with the oil and continue cooking, tossing occasionally, just until coated and crisp.

Ladle gazpacho into soup bowls and sprinkle each with some of the cucumber, chives and croutons. Serve immediately.

Fresh Produce

Why does food taste so great in Italy, France and Spain? Well, nothing beats produce that has come straight from the field to the kitchen. It's seasonal, fresh and delicious, and that makes all the difference. Using local produce in season is fundamental to Mediterranean cuisine. In North America, we tend toward a 24/7 mindset, expecting all ingredients to be available all the time. But as a result, our taste buds often suffer. The simple tomato and bocconcini salad we make in Vancouver in November isn't like the one we had in Verona in September, because hothouse tomatoes cannot compare to field-ripened ones.

Of course, you don't have to go to Spain or Italy for good food, but you do need to consider the origins of your ingredients. I have always been passionate about freshness and flavour – great ingredients are crucial to end results. In this country, we're blessed with wonderful local ingredients, and enjoying them as they arrive at the market is one way of celebrating the turn of the seasons.

Roasted Red Pepper Soup with Chèvre and Shiso

In the late summer, when peppers are plentiful and cheap, I make large batches of this soup and freeze it to enjoy in the winter. It has a great texture and a bit of a kick thanks to the chili oil. Shiso, an herb with a bright, sweet flavour, adds a fresh note. It comes from the same family as basil and mint. Fresh basil would be a good substitute if shiso is unavailable.

Makes 6 servings

6 sweet red peppers
1/4 cup (50 mL) extra-virgin olive oil
1 cup (250 mL) chopped red onion
2 tbsp (30 mL) minced jalapeño pepper
    (including some of the seeds if you want extra heat)
2 cloves garlic, minced
1 tsp (5 mL) ground cumin
1 tsp (5 mL) sea salt
1/2 tsp (2 mL) freshly ground pepper
1/4 cup (50 mL) all-purpose flour
5 to 6 cups (1.25 to 1.5 L) chicken stock
2 roma tomatoes, seeded and chopped
1 tbsp (15 mL) tomato paste
Sea salt and freshly ground pepper
2 tbsp (30 mL) chili oil
4 oz (125 g) chèvre, crumbled
2 shiso leaves, shredded

Preheat the broiler. Roast the whole red peppers under the broiler (or over an open flame on a gas stove) until the skin blackens and chars. Place in a bowl and let cool. Peel off the blackened skin and discard. Cut the peppers in half; remove the seeds and core. Chop peppers coarsely.

In a heavy saucepan, heat the oil over medium heat; add the onion, jalapeño, garlic, cumin, salt and pepper. Reduce heat to low and sauté until vegetables are soft, 5 to 7 minutes. Add the flour; cook over low heat, stirring, until flour is cooked, about 5 minutes.

Add 5 cups (1.125 L) chicken stock, the roasted peppers, tomatoes and tomato paste. Increase heat to medium and cook for 30 minutes. Let cool. Transfer to a blender or food processor and purée. Return to the pan and season to taste with more salt and pepper. Thin with more chicken stock, if necessary. Ladle into bowls and drizzle with chili oil. Top with the chèvre and shiso.

Roasted Pumpkin Soup with Cumin Cream

Although pumpkin is probably the most widely known member of the squash family, it's underappreciated – its use has been limited almost exclusively to pies and jack-o'-lanterns. Now, much to my delight, it's showing up in pastas, soups and desserts. Here, the pumpkin will take a bit of time to prepare; plan on 10 to 15 minutes. The results are worth it – a gorgeous fall colour and rich flavour.

Makes 8 servings

1 small to medium pumpkin
3/4 tsp (4 mL) freshly grated nutmeg
4 tbsp (60 mL) butter
1 clove garlic, minced
1 onion, minced
1 large leek (white part only), coarsely chopped
1 quart (1 L) chicken stock
1/2 cup (125 mL) light cream
Sea salt and freshly ground white pepper

Cumin Cream:
1/3 cup (75 mL) heavy cream
1/2 tsp (2 mL) ground cumin

Preheat the oven to 375°F (190°C).

Peel, seed and cut the pumpkin into 1-inch (2.5 cm) cubes and place in roasting pan; sprinkle with 1/4 tsp (1 mL) of the nutmeg. Roast until soft and golden, 30 to 40 minutes.

In 4- to 6-quart (4 to 6 L) stockpot, heat the butter over medium heat; sauté the garlic, onion and leek until softened, about 5 minutes. Add the cooked pumpkin and stock; bring to a boil. Reduce heat and simmer until tender, about 15 minutes. In a food processor fitted with a metal blade, purée the pumpkin mixture in 2-cup (500 mL) batches until smooth. Return the purée to the stockpot. Stir in the cream, remaining nutmeg, and salt and white pepper to taste. If necessary (depending on the size of pumpkin used), add a bit of water to thin the soup to the desired consistency.

Cumin Cream: In a bowl, whip the cream with the cumin until soft peaks form.

Ladle soup into bowls and garnish with a dollop of Cumin Cream.

"Wet" Coast Seafood Chowder

When it comes to seafood, we're totally spoiled on the "wet" West Coast. We have ready access to incredible salmon, crab, halibut, clams – the list goes on. This chowder is a big hit in our storefront. Customers choose it to ward off the effects of cold, damp winter days. For lunch or a light dinner, serve this with the Crackling Cheddar Cornbread, page 62.

Makes 6 to 8 servings

4 tbsp (60 mL) unsalted butter
1 large sweet white onion, finely chopped
1 stalk celery, finely chopped
1 1/2 tsp (7 mL) sea salt
1 tsp (5 mL) dried thyme
Freshly ground pepper
2 cups (500 mL) cubed (about 1 inch/2.5 cm)
    red-skinned potatoes
3 cups (750 mL) heavy cream
1 cup (250 mL) milk
3/4 lb (375 g) hot-smoked wild salmon, cut into
    1 1/2-inch (3.5 cm) chunks
1/4 lb (125 g) scallops
1/3 lb (170 g) fresh-cooked hand-peeled baby shrimp
    or Dungeness crabmeat

In a heavy sauté pan, melt the butter over medium-low heat; cook the onion and celery until soft but not brown. Remove from heat and add the salt, thyme, and pepper to taste.

In a saucepan, cover the potatoes with cold water and cook just until they can be pierced easily with a knife. Drain.

In a 4- to 6-quart (4 to 6 L) stockpot or Dutch oven over medium-low heat, combine the sautéed onion mixture, potatoes, cream and milk and heat through (do not let the mixture come to a boil). Add the salmon and scallops and cook for 2 to 3 minutes. Do not let mixture come to a boil or it could separate. Add the shrimp; heat through and serve.

Shrimp Bruschetta with Red Pepper Aïoli (page 12)

Spicy Smoked Salmon Corn Cakes with Crème Fraîche (page 24)

Grilled Asparagus Salad with Warm Sourdough Croutons and Cilantro Dressing (page 40)

Grilled Salmon, Wild Rice and Arugula Salad with Watercress Vinaigrette (page 50)

Pizza with Caramelized Onions and Cambozola (page 60)

Summer Spaghettini with Fresh Corn and Grape Tomatoes (page 69)

Veal Chops with Sun-Dried Tomato and Basil (page 83)

G.L. Lamb Burgers with Feta Mayonnaise and Mint (page 96)

Vichyssoise with Dungeness Crab and Frizzled Leeks

Vichyssoise is basically cold potato soup, but what makes it so ambrosial is the texture and the seasoning. Using a blender instead of a food processor will give you far superior results; it will be much smoother, which is the goal here. If you don't have a blender, use a food processor, then strain the mixture through a sieve.

Makes 6 servings

3 leeks, washed thoroughly
1 1/2 tbsp (22 mL) butter
3 russet potatoes, peeled and cut into 1-inch (2.5 cm) cubes
2 1/2 cups (625 mL) chicken stock
1 1/2 cups (375 mL) light cream
1 tbsp (15 mL) fresh lemon juice
Sea salt and freshly ground white pepper
4 oz (125 g) fresh crabmeat

Frizzled Leeks:
2 cups (500 mL) grape seed oil or peanut oil
1 large leek, washed, dried and cut into very thin lengthwise strips

Trim the leeks, leaving the white part and about 1 inch (2.5 cm) of the green. Slice as thinly as possible. In a heavy sauté pan, melt the butter over low heat; cook the leeks until soft but not letting them colour. Add the potatoes and stock and simmer until soft. Let cool. Transfer to a blender and purée until very smooth. Add the cream, lemon juice, and salt and white pepper to taste. Refrigerate until chilled. Taste and adjust seasoning to serve.

Frizzled Leeks: In a saucepan, carefully heat the oil over medium-high until hot. Add the leek strips and cook until crispy, about 1 to 2 minutes. Transfer to a paper towel–lined plate to drain.

To serve, place a small amount of the crabmeat in each soup plate. Ladle the soup around the crab and garnish with Frizzled Leeks.

Greens with Roasted Figs and Gorgonzola

I love the combination of flavours in this dish. The bitter greens play off the salty Gorgonzola and the sweetness of the figs. It's a great salad to enjoy after an entrée – you can get your salad course and cheese course all in one. If Gorgonzola isn't available, substitute another blue cheese; Saint Agur, Cambozola or Fourme d'Amber work well.

Makes 6 servings

2 heads radicchio, cut in half
1 head frisée, washed and torn
2 Belgian endives, cut in half, core removed and sliced lengthwise
1⁄4 cup (50 mL) red wine vinegar
1 tsp (5 mL) Dijon mustard
1 cup (250 mL) extra-virgin olive oil
Sea salt and freshly ground pepper
12 dried figs, preferably Calimyrna or Mission, cut in half
   and stems removed
4 oz (125 g) Gorgonzola, crumbled

Preheat the barbecue to medium-high; grill the radicchio, cut side down, until grill marks appear, about 3 minutes. The leaves will turn a bit brown, but that's fine. Break apart the radicchio heads and combine with the frisée and endive strips. Set aside.

In a bowl, whisk together the vinegar and mustard. Gradually add the oil, whisking, until the dressing comes together and emulsifies. Season to taste with salt and pepper.

Preheat the oven to 350°F (180°C). Gently toss the figs with 1/4 cup (50 mL) of the vinaigrette and place on a baking sheet. Roast until heated through and slightly caramelized, about 10 minutes. Transfer to a plate. Set aside.

Toss the greens with enough of the remaining vinaigrette to coat. Divide the salad among serving plates. Sprinkle with the Gorgonzola. Arrange the figs around the rim of each plate to serve.

Pear and Endive Salad with Stilton Cheese and Lemon Dressing

This is my favourite winter salad, hands down. We served it at small catered events, but we've never sold it in the store, because the pears and endive both brown far too quickly when sitting. That said, you can have everything prepped and ready to go and simply slice the pears and endive close to the time of serving. Whole Belgian endive keeps very well in the refrigerator, especially if you wrap it in a paper towel and plastic wrap.

Make sure your pears are at room temperature to give the most flavour. Experiment with different varieties. Anjou, Bartlett and Bosc are most readily available, but if you can get your hands on any others, go for it. You could also try apples instead of pears and replace the pecans with hazelnuts or walnuts (walnuts go rancid very quickly, so make sure you buy them from a reliable source where they haven't been sitting on the shelf for a long time).

Makes 6 servings

4 Belgian endives, halved and cored
1 ripe pear, Anjou or Bartlett
6 oz (180 g) Stilton cheese, crumbled
1 oz (30 g) toasted pecan halves
1 tbsp (15 mL) finely chopped chives

Lemon Dressing:
2 tsp (10 mL) grated lemon zest
3 tbsp (45 mL) fresh lemon juice
1 tsp (5 mL) liquid honey
1 tsp (5 mL) Dijon mustard
Sea salt and freshly ground pepper
1/2 cup (125 mL) olive oil or hazelnut oil

Slice the endives as thinly as possible and place in a large bowl. Cut the pear into quarters, removing core. Cut the quarters into long, thin slices and add to the bowl.

Lemon Dressing: Whisk together the lemon zest and juice, honey, mustard, and salt and pepper to taste. Gradually whisk in the oil until creamy.

Toss the salad with the dressing. Divide the salad among 6 plates. Top each with the Stilton, pecans and chives. Serve immediately.

Grilled Asparagus Salad with Warm Sourdough Croutons and Cilantro Dressing

Asparagus is the sophisticated, sexy member of the vegetable family, adding allure to any meal. It used to be available only in the late spring and early summer, but has become almost as ubiquitous as carrots and broccoli. Grilling the asparagus adds visual interest to this dish, but you could also blanch the spears in boiling water for a minute or two. Make sure you cook them enough to take the crunch away; they should be just crisp.

Makes 6 servings

6 thick slices sourdough bread, crusts removed
1/3 cup (75 mL) extra-virgin olive oil
1 lb (500 g) jumbo asparagus spears
Sea salt and freshly ground pepper
4 oz (125 g) Parmesan cheese, shaved
3 tbsp (45 mL) chopped chives

Cilantro Dressing:
2 tsp (10 mL) cumin seeds
1/4 cup (50 mL) orange juice concentrate
1 cup (250 mL) fresh cilantro leaves
1/2 cup (125 mL) grape seed or vegetable oil
1 tbsp (15 mL) fresh lemon juice
1 tbsp (15 mL) mayonnaise
Sea salt and cayenne pepper

Preheat the barbecue or broiler to medium-high.

Brush the bread slices with 1/4 cup (50 mL) of the oil and grill until golden brown. Cut the slices into 1 1/2-inch (3.5 cm) cubes and set aside.

Toss the asparagus with the remaining oil, and salt and pepper to taste. Place on the grill and cook until char marks appear and asparagus is slightly blackened, about 4 minutes. Let cool.

Cilantro Dressing: Toast the cumin seeds in a dry heavy skillet over medium heat for 4 minutes. Grind the seeds with a mortar and pestle or in a spice mill. In a blender or food processor, purée the orange juice concentrate and cilantro until smooth. Add the oil, lemon juice and cumin; mix well. Add the mayonnaise and mix well. Season to taste with salt and cayenne pepper.

Pile the asparagus on a plate with all the tips at one end. Drizzle with 1/4 cup (50 mL) of the Cilantro Dressing and garnish with the Parmesan cheese, croutons and chives. Season to taste with pepper. Serve remaining dressing on the side.

Pastel Fruit Salad with Lemon Verbena

The lovely pale pastels make this an unusual fruit salad. If you can't find lemon verbena, use lemon balm or mint. However, if you can't find yellow watermelon, don't substitute pink – it spoils the colour effect.

Makes 8 servings

2 kiwis, peeled and diced
1/4 honeydew, melon balled
1/8 yellow watermelon, diced
1/4 cantaloupe, melon balled
1/2 pineapple, cut into chunks
1/2 papaya, diced
1/4 lb (125 g) green grapes or golden raspberries
2 tsp (10 mL) liquid honey
1/4 cup (50 mL) freshly squeezed orange juice
Grated zest of 1 lemon
2 tbsp (30 mL) chopped lemon verbena

In a large bowl, toss together the kiwi, honeydew, watermelon, cantaloupe, pineapple, papaya and grapes.

In a small saucepan, heat the honey over low heat to thin it slightly; remove from heat and stir in the orange juice and lemon zest. Let cool to room temperature; pour over the fruit. Toss gently and sprinkle with the lemon verbena.

Barbecued Pork Tenderloin, Barley Pilaf and Grilled Sweet Corn Salad with Red Wine Basil Vinaigrette

The rich flavour of the marinated pork tenderloin in this dish plays well against the tender barley and sweet corn. If you're pressed for time, pick up a barbecued pork tenderloin from your favourite Chinese takeout or Asian butcher. This salad transports well to the beach, the boat, or even stuffed into a knapsack for that hike up Whistler. You can replace the pork tenderloin with grilled chicken, or skip the barley and add skinny green beans.

Makes 6 servings

1 cup (250 mL) soy sauce
1/2 cup (125 mL) packed golden brown sugar
1/4 cup (50 mL) rye whisky
1 pork tenderloin, about 1 lb (500 g)
4 cobs corn, husked
1 tsp (5 mL) sea salt
3/4 cup (175 mL) pearl barley
2 green onions, thinly sliced
1/4 cup (50 mL) minced chives
3/4 cup (175 mL) cherry tomatoes, halved
1 sweet red pepper, diced
1/3 lb (170 g) smoked mozzarella, shredded
Sea salt and freshly ground pepper

Red Wine Basil Vinaigrette:
1 tbsp (15 mL) red wine vinegar
2 tsp (10 mL) chopped fresh basil
1/2 tsp (2 mL) Dijon mustard
1/2 tsp (2 mL) minced garlic
3 oz (90 mL) olive oil
Sea salt and freshly ground pepper

In a flat shallow dish, whisk together the soy sauce, brown sugar and whisky. Place the pork tenderloin in the marinade; cover and refrigerate for at least 2 hours or overnight.

Preheat the barbecue to medium-high and grill the pork tenderloin until just a hint of pink remains inside, about 10 minutes per side. Transfer to a cutting board and let rest for at least 15 minutes. Slice thinly and set aside.

Place the corn cobs on the preheated barbecue and cook until grill-marked on all sides and tender-crisp, about 10 minutes. Let cool. Cut the kernels off each cob and set aside.

In a large saucepan, bring 1 1/2 cups (375 mL) water and salt to a boil; cook the barley, stirring, until it returns to the boil. Reduce heat to simmer, cover and cook until barley is soft but chewy, about 30 minutes. Drain, rinse with cold water and drain again; set aside.

Red Wine Basil Vinaigrette: In a bowl, whisk together the vinegar, basil, mustard and garlic. Whisk in the oil until the dressing comes together and emulsifies. Season to taste with salt and pepper.

In a large bowl, combine the green onions, chives, tomatoes, red pepper, cheese, corn, barley and sliced pork; pour in the vinaigrette and toss. Season to taste with salt and pepper.

Grilled Potato Salad with Crispy Pancetta, Green Beans and Lemon Dijon Vinaigrette

The first time I heard of someone grilling potatoes I thought it seemed a bit strange, but now it's one of my favourite ways to serve them in the summer. This is a gutsy salad, with the tarragon and capers adding a sharp contrast to the richness of the pancetta and walnuts. Serve it with a rib-eye or New York strip loin and a good bottle of Zinfandel.

Makes 6 servings

4 lb (2 kg) small red potatoes, cut in half
1 tbsp (15 mL) olive oil
1/2 lb (250 g) green beans, stems removed
2/3 cup (150 mL) walnuts
6 slices pancetta
2 tbsp (30 mL) capers, drained
1/4 cup (50 mL) chopped fresh tarragon
Sea salt and freshly ground pepper

Lemon Dijon Vinaigrette:
1/4 cup (50 mL) fresh lemon juice
1 tbsp (15 mL) Dijon mustard
1 large clove garlic, crushed
3/4 cup (175 mL) olive oil
Sea salt and freshly ground pepper

Preheat the barbecue.

In a saucepan over high heat, cover the potatoes with cold water; bring to a boil. Cook until tender. Drain and toss with the oil while the potatoes are still warm. Transfer potatoes to the grill and cook, cut side down, until grill-marked, 4 to 5 minutes. Set aside.

Bring a saucepan of water to a boil over high heat. Add the green beans and simmer for 1 minute. Drain and rinse with cold water; drain again. Set aside.

Preheat the oven to 350°F (180°C). Place the walnuts on a baking sheet and toast in the oven until golden but not brown, 5 to 10 minutes. Let cool.

Place the pancetta slices in a cold sauté pan. Turn heat to medium-high and cook until crispy, about 3 minutes. Let cool, then crumble.

Lemon Dijon Vinaigrette: In a small bowl, whisk together the lemon juice, mustard and garlic. Whisking constantly, dribble in the oil until the mixture comes together and emulsifies. Season to taste with salt and pepper.

In a large bowl, combine the potatoes, beans, walnuts, capers, tarragon and 1 cup (250 mL) of the vinaigrette; toss to coat. Season to taste with salt and pepper. Sprinkle with the crumbled pancetta.

Roasted Yam and Yukon Gold Potato Salad with Mizuna and Cider Vinaigrette

At LSFF, we started using mizuna about five years ago. We wanted a salad green that was interesting but not quite as bitter or peppery as arugula. Mizuna may be hard to find, although it's easy to grow if you have any spare room in your garden. Substitute arugula, baby spinach or mustard greens if necessary. This salad does not keep well once tossed with the vinaigrette, so don't dress it until just before serving.

Makes 6 servings

1/2 lb (250 g) yams
1 lb (500 g) Yukon Gold potatoes
1 tbsp (15 mL) olive oil
4 slices bacon, chopped into 1/2-inch (1 cm) pieces
1/4 lb (125 g) mizuna greens
1 tbsp (15 mL) minced chives
Sea salt and freshly ground pepper

Cider Vinaigrette:
2 tbsp (30 mL) cider vinegar
2 tsp (10 mL) liquid honey
1 tsp (5 mL) Dijon mustard
1/3 cup (75 mL) olive oil

Preheat the oven to 375°F (190°C). Peel the yams and potatoes and cut into 2-inch (5 cm) chunks. Toss with the oil and roast until tender, 25 to 30 minutes. Meanwhile, in a skillet, fry the bacon pieces until crispy. Set aside.

Cider Vinaigrette: In a bowl, whisk together the vinegar, honey and mustard. Whisk in the oil drop by drop until the mixture begins to emulsify. As mixture thickens, you can add the oil more quickly, continuing to whisk to bring it together.

In a bowl, toss the warm yams and potatoes with vinaigrette. Add the bacon, mizuna and chives; toss again. Season to taste with salt and pepper. Serve immediately.

Positano Penne Salad
with Lemon Balsamic Vinaigrette

With their rise in popularity, sometimes pasta salads have been abused, giving them a bad reputation. Often the pasta is overcooked, overdressed and under-seasoned. This recipe will restore your faith in pasta salad. Serve it with grilled chicken or fish that has been drizzled with lemon juice, oil and fresh herbs.

Makes 6 servings

Sea salt
1 lb (500 g) penne
1 sweet red pepper, julienned
1 sweet yellow pepper, julienned
1 cup (250 mL) cherry tomatoes, halved
1 cucumber, diced
1/2 small red onion, thinly sliced
1/2 cup (125 mL) niçoise or kalamata olives
1/2 cup (125 mL) pine nuts, toasted
3 tbsp (45 mL) thinly shredded fresh basil
2 tbsp (30 mL) thinly shredded fresh mint
1/2 lb (250 g) feta cheese, crumbled
Sea salt and freshly ground pepper

Lemon Balsamic Vinaigrette:
Grated zest of 2 lemons, finely chopped
1/4 cup (50 mL) balsamic vinegar
3/4 cup (175 mL) olive oil
Sea salt and freshly ground pepper

In a large pot, bring 4 quarts (4 L) water to a boil with 1 tbsp (15 mL) salt. Add the penne, stirring until it comes back to the boil; cook until al dente, about 10 minutes. Drain and rinse with cold water.

Lemon Balsamic Vinaigrette: In a bowl, combine the lemon zest and vinegar. Whisk in the oil and season to taste with salt and pepper.

Place pasta in a large bowl. Add the red and yellow peppers, cherry tomatoes, cucumber, onion, olives, pine nuts, basil and mint. Drizzle with the vinaigrette and toss to coat. Season to taste with salt and pepper. Sprinkle with the feta. Serve at room temperature.

Grilled Chicken Polenta Salad with Asiago and White Wine Dijon Vinaigrette

This is one of my all-time favourite summer chicken salads. The idea originally came from the Oakville Grocer in California's Napa Valley, a store that serves up mountains of salads, deli meats and amazing cheeses to people wanting a picnic in between wine tastings.

After one visit, I was inspired to create this recipe upon returning to Vancouver. Although it's a bit of work to make the polenta, you'll love the results.

Makes 6 to 8 servings

Polenta:
1 1/4 cups (300 mL) quick-cooking polenta
1 cup (250 mL) shredded aged cheddar cheese
1/2 cup (125 mL) sour cream
1/2 large bunch fresh parsley, chopped
4 tsp (20 mL) salt
2 1/4 tsp (11 mL) freshly ground pepper

Salad:
4 boneless skinless chicken breasts
1 tsp (5 mL) olive oil
Sea salt and freshly ground pepper
1 sweet red pepper, cut into 1-inch (2.5 cm) cubes
2 stalks celery, diced
1/2 cup (125 mL) grated Asiago cheese
1/4 red onion, cut into 1/2-inch (1 cm) dice
1 tbsp (15 mL) finely chopped chives
Sea salt and freshly ground pepper

White Wine Dijon Vinaigrette:
1/3 cup (75 mL) white wine vinegar
2 tsp (10 mL) Dijon mustard
1/2 tsp (2 mL) sugar
1/2 cup (125 mL) vegetable oil
1/2 cup (125 mL) olive oil
Salt and freshly ground pepper

Polenta: In a large saucepan, bring 4 1/2 cups (1.125 L) water to a boil. Add the polenta in a slow, steady stream, whisking. Boil gently for 5 to 7 minutes, stirring constantly. Lower the heat to medium, stir in the cheese, sour cream, parsley, salt and pepper and cook for 5 to 7 minutes longer. Pour the mixture onto a parchment paper–lined cookie sheet and let cool until firm. Turn out onto a chopping board and cut into 1-inch (2.5 cm) cubes. Set aside.

Salad: Preheat the barbecue to medium-high. Drizzle the chicken breasts with the oil and sprinkle with salt and pepper. Place on the grill and cook, turning once or twice, until juices run clear when chicken is pierced, 7 to 10 minutes. Remove from heat and let cool for 15 minutes. Cut into small cubes. Set aside.

White Wine Dijon Vinaigrette: In a bowl, whisk together the vinegar, mustard and sugar. Whisk together the vegetable and olive oils and dribble into vinegar mixture, whisking constantly until dressing comes together and emulsifies. Season to taste with salt and pepper. Use immediately or refrigerate until using.

In a large bowl, combine the chicken cubes, red pepper, celery, cheese and onion; toss together gently. Add the chives and polenta and toss again just until combined. Drizzle in the vinaigrette, starting with 1/2 cup (125 mL) and adding more if salad isn't moist enough. Season to taste with salt and pepper.

Grilled Salmon, Wild Rice and Arugula Salad with Watercress Vinaigrette

We used to pack dozens of picnic baskets during the summer months, and this salad was one of our most requested. It's delicious and beautiful to look at, with the pale pink salmon, watercress and wild rice. Add some focaccia or Raincoast Crisps and a glass of Pinot Gris for a brilliant lunch.

Makes 8 servings

Sea salt
2 cups (500 mL) orzo pasta
2 cups (500 mL) wild rice
1 3/4 lb (875 g) salmon fillet
Olive oil
1 bunch young arugula or mustard greens, torn into 2-inch (5 cm) lengths
1/2 cup (125 mL) chopped fresh dill
1/4 cup (50 mL) capers, drained
1 small red onion, minced
2 tsp (10 mL) grated lemon zest
Freshly ground pepper

Watercress Vinaigrette:
1/4 cup (50 mL) white wine vinegar
1 tbsp (15 mL) chopped watercress
1 tsp (5 mL) grainy mustard
3/4 cup (175 mL) olive oil
Sea salt and freshly ground pepper

Bring a large pot of water and 1 tbsp (15 mL) salt to boil. Stir in the orzo and return to a boil. Cook until al dente, 8 to 10 minutes. Drain, rinse with cold water and drain again. Set aside.

Wash the wild rice. Bring 4 cups (1 L) water and 1/2 tsp (2 mL) salt to a boil. Add the rice, stirring as it returns to a boil. Reduce heat, cover and simmer just until grains of rice pop, 40 to 45 minutes. Drain, rinse with cold water and drain again. Set aside.

Oil the barbecue and preheat to medium-high. Brush both sides of the salmon with oil; sprinkle with salt. Place the salmon on the grill; close the lid and cook for 4 minutes. Turn salmon and cook until it's opaque and flakes easily with fork, 2 to 4 minutes longer. Remove from heat and let cool.

Watercress Vinaigrette: In a blender, combine the vinegar, watercress and mustard. Dribble in the oil, blending until dressing comes together and emulsifies. Season to taste with salt and pepper.

In a large bowl, combine the orzo, rice, arugula, dill, capers, onion and lemon zest. Toss with enough of the vinaigrette to coat. Break salmon into large chunks and gently stir into the salad. Season to taste with salt and pepper.

Behind the Scenes at Lesley Stowe Fine Foods

When I opened Lesley Stowe Fine Foods, it was my mission to bring specialty products to Vancouver and, at the same time, educate consumers about why one would buy artisanal bread made from a natural starter or cook with extra-virgin olive oil from a single estate or eat unpasteurized cheese. North Americans, accustomed to what the chain stores offered, were caught up in a wave of convenience food. Cooking classes made the products we carried more accessible and desirable, as we demonstrated how and why great ingredients make a difference.

Although we're now focused on producing Raincoast Crisps, we continue to sell specialty groceries and signature products from our boutique. We stock everything from decadent chocolate brownies and organic coffee to perfectly ripe Brie de Meaux, seafood fusilli and truffle oil. Our clientele is enormously varied: women who love to cook and seek out the best products, young men who sell skateboards (there are a bunch of board shops nearby), designers who appreciate delicious food beautifully presented, bachelors who want to impress, and professional chefs looking for a hard-to-find ingredient. If you love to cook and eat, you have to visit LSFF.

Summer Pepper Slaw with Ginger Sesame Vinaigrette

Don't let the reference to summer in this recipe's title stop you from making it in the winter. Most of these peppers are available year-round; if you can't find one of the colours, just add more of another. The Ginger Sesame Vinaigrette recipe will make more than you need for the slaw, but it can be kept in the refrigerator for up to a month. Use it as a marinade for pork tenderloin or flank steak or toss it on salad greens with fresh-cooked hand-peeled baby shrimp.

Makes 6 to 8 servings

1 small sweet red pepper
1 small sweet orange pepper
1 small sweet yellow pepper
1 small sweet purple pepper
1/4 red onion
1 jalapeño pepper
Sea salt and freshly ground pepper

Ginger Sesame Vinaigrette:
1 piece (1/4-inch/5 mm) fresh gingerroot, peeled and minced
1 large clove garlic, minced
1/4 cup (50 mL) fresh lemon juice
4 tsp (20 mL) soy sauce
1 tbsp (15 mL) liquid honey
1 tbsp (15 mL) sherry
2 tsp (10 mL) sambal oelek or chili sauce
1 cup (250 mL) grape seed or vegetable oil
1/3 cup (75 mL) toasted sesame seeds

Core and seed the red, orange, yellow and purple peppers. Slice into thin julienne strips. Cut the onion in half with the grain; peel back the skin of the onion and cut lengthwise into 1/4-inch (5 mm) strips. Core, seed and finely dice the jalapeño pepper. (Depending on your heat tolerance, you can add a few of the seeds.) In a bowl, toss together the peppers, jalapeño pepper and onion. Set aside.

Ginger Sesame Vinaigrette: In a bowl, whisk together the gingerroot, garlic, lemon juice, soy sauce, honey, sherry and sambal oelek. Gradually whisk in the oil. Add the sesame seeds.

Add 1/2 cup (125 mL) of the vinaigrette to the pepper mixture and toss to coat. Season to taste with salt and pepper. Serve at room temperature.

Low-Fat Mango Vinaigrette

Here's a vinaigrette that's perfect for all those chicken and seafood salads you make in the summer. As you see, there's no oil in this vinaigrette, so you can indulge in this without guilt during bathing suit season. Make sure the mango is ripe.

Makes 2 cups (500 mL)

1 large ripe mango
Juice of 3 oranges
2 tbsp (30 mL) fresh lemon juice
1/3 cup (75 mL) passion fruit juice
3 tbsp (45 mL) raspberry vinegar
Pinch each ground cloves, ground ginger, cayenne pepper and sea salt

Cut mango flesh (see How to Cut a Mango, below) and scoop into a food processor. Purée the mango until smooth. Add the orange, lemon and passion fruit juices, vinegar, cloves, ginger, cayenne and salt. Taste and adjust seasoning. Refrigerate until ready to use.

How to Cut a Mango Cutting about 1/4 inch (5 mm) off the centre (to avoid pit), halve the mango lengthwise. Cut the pit away from the other half. Using a sharp paring knife (mangoes are very fibrous, so sharp is key) and holding one of the mango halves in the palm of your hand, make lengthwise cuts, about 1/4 inch (5 mm) apart, into the fruit through to the skin (but not your skin!). Repeat this process crosswise to form a grid pattern. Using a large metal spoon, scoop the flesh out of the skin. Repeat with the other mango half. This process may seem involved but once you have done it, you'll see it really is much easier and less messy than peeling the mango.

Balsamic Caesar Dressing

Caesar is still the most popular salad on most restaurant menus, and everyone wants a good recipe they can make at home. This dressing has a little twist: it calls for balsamic vinegar in place of the traditional red wine vinegar.

Makes 1 1/2 cups (375 mL)

2 tbsp (30 mL) fresh lemon juice
4 tsp (20 mL) balsamic vinegar
1 tsp (5 mL) Worcestershire sauce
1/2 tsp (2 mL) Tabasco sauce
1 tsp (5 mL) Dijon mustard
1/2 tsp (2 mL) freshly ground pepper
1 egg
2 cloves garlic
2 anchovies
1 cup (250 mL) olive oil
Sea salt

In a food processor, combine the lemon juice, vinegar, Worcestershire and Tabasco sauces, mustard, pepper, egg, garlic and anchovies; process until well mixed. Gradually add the oil, processing until emulsified. Season to taste with salt. Refrigerate until using. The dressing can be refrigerated for up to 1 week.

Chapter Three

PIZZAS, PASTAS & GRAINS

A crisp pizza crust is the perfect blank canvas for an inspired creation. Likewise, freshly cooked pasta – so delicious with any of a myriad of sauces, from simple fresh corn and tomatoes to more exotic combinations.

Pizza is one of my favourite ways to get people – especially children – involved in cooking. Once you've made the dough, the topping possibilities are endless. I don't want to sound like a broken record, but keep your choices selective, as we did in this chapter. I've listed some combinations I like best. To make your life simple, double your pizza dough and freeze half. Then dinner's ready pronto the next time you want pizza. Another option is to make calzones, which are basically pizzas folded in half so you have a giant turnover. Pinch the edges together over the filling, bake and you have a little bit of heaven.

Pasta was the food of choice for most of us until the '90s, when the whole fear of carbohydrates put the pasta and bread industries into a tailspin. Sales dropped dramatically as low-carb shops started popping up all over, promoting everything from bread and pasta to baked goods with low or no carbohydrates. Then we saw the light and realized that everything in moderation was a much more sensible and realistic approach. At LSFF, pasta and grain dishes have always played an important role on our menu. Even when people were trying to avoid carbohydrates, they couldn't resist our Summer Spaghettini with Fresh Corn and Grape Tomatoes or our Wild Rice, Lentils and Pearl Barley with Toasted Pine Nuts. One of the great things about pasta is that there are so many shapes available. The Italians are geniuses when it comes to the possibilities, from rice-shaped orzo pasta to orrechiette, the playful "little ears" that are perfect for trapping sauce. Polenta, another one of those misunderstood starches, has come onto the North American culinary scene recently. In its simplest form, polenta is basically cornmeal, salt and water, but here's where the fun starts: try adding fresh herbs and cream or butter and Parmesan cheese. You can serve it soft with a meat sauce on top or pour it onto a baking sheet, cut it into shapes, then grill or fry it. Or use it as a base for hors d'oeuvres or for replacing pasta layers. Think of these recipes as a blueprint to be played with.

Pizza Dough

This recipe will make enough for two large pizzas the size of a baking sheet, so you can bake one and pop the other in the freezer for future use. I would highly recommend using a pizza stone; the crust will be much crisper. I actually keep my stone in the oven on the bottom rack all the time, so I don't have to haul it in and out. Once you're in the swing of making pizza, it will become a favourite in your house. There are so many topping combinations – only your imagination will limit you. A note of caution from the Italians: don't mix too many flavours; try to limit yourself to three.

Makes enough for 2 pizzas

1 1/2 cups (375 mL) warm water
1 pkg (2 1/2 tsp/12 mL) active dry yeast
Pinch sugar
5 cups (1.25 L) all-purpose flour
1/3 cup (75 mL) olive oil
1/2 tsp (2 mL) sea salt

In a small bowl, combine the warm water, yeast and sugar. Let stand for 5 minutes. Transfer to a mixing bowl and stir in the flour, oil and salt. Using an electric mixer on low speed, mix for 5 minutes.

Turn out the dough onto a floured board and knead for several minutes, adding additional flour only as necessary to keep the dough from sticking. When the dough is smooth and shiny, transfer it to a bowl that has been brushed with olive oil. To prevent a skin from forming, brush the top of the dough with additional olive oil. Cover with plastic wrap and let rise in a warm, draft-free place until doubled in bulk, 1 1/2 to 2 hours. Punch down the dough and knead once more. If sticky, knead in a bit more flour.

Preheat the oven to 400°F (200°C).

To Bake Pizza: Roll out the dough to 1/4-inch (5 mm) thickness. The thinner the dough, the crisper the end result will be. Remember, round pizzas start from round balls. If you have no rolling pin, use your fingers to push the dough into a circle. Line a baking sheet with parchment paper or sprinkle it with cornmeal (this will make it easier to serve the pizza after baking). Place pizza base on baking sheet and add toppings. Bake until the bottom begins to brown, about 15 minutes (lift it with a spatula to check). After baking, brush the edges with olive oil and sprinkle with fresh herbs for a fresh, appetizing look.

Pizza with Caramelized Onions and Cambozola

This is a marriage that will stand the test of time: sweet caramelized onions are the perfect backdrop for the salty flavour and creamy texture of Cambozola. If you like a little crunch, sprinkle on some pine nuts. Be careful not to load the onions too thickly or else the dough won't cook properly. This makes enough topping for one pizza (half the dough recipe on page 59). You can easily double the topping quantities if you're feeding a crowd.

Makes 6 servings

2 large red onions
1 tbsp (15 mL) olive oil
1/4 cup (50 mL) balsamic vinegar
1 pizza base (1/2 Pizza Dough recipe, page 59)
6 oz (180 g) Cambozola, cut into 1/2-inch (1 cm) thick squares

Preheat the oven to 400°F (200°C).

Cut the onion into 1/4-inch (5 mm) wedges. In a skillet, heat the oil over medium heat; sauté the onions until softened. Add the vinegar and cook until all the liquid is absorbed.

Remove from heat and let cool. Spread the onion mixture over the pizza base and top evenly with pieces of Camobozola. Bake for 15 minutes, until crust is golden and cheese is melted.

Don't Drown Your Pizza!

North Americans seem to feel a great temptation to load their pizzas with too many toppings. Pizza tends to taste better if you don't empty your fridge when making it. So take a tip from the Italians and keep a light hand. That way, the flavours will shine through, and you won't end up with a soggy crust.

Here are some of my favourite pizza combinations:

sweet red peppers, red onion, kalamata olives, tomatoes, crumbled feta cheese and fresh oregano

smoked salmon, capers, red onion and chèvre

roasted potato slices, pancetta, sweet white onion slivers and grated Gruyère cheese

plum tomato, bocconcini and basil

leek, brie and portobello mushrooms

grilled chicken, spinach, oven-dried tomatoes and Boursin cheese

chorizo sausage, sweet red pepper and Asiago cheese

roasted Japanese eggplant, ricotta and mint leaves

shrimp, fennel and crème fraîche

roasted garlic, zucchini, olive oil and pecorino cheese

Crackling Cheddar Cornbread

This is perfect to serve with your favourite chili or soup. You can easily alter the recipe by omitting the bacon or cheddar and adding finely diced jalapeño pepper or sun-dried tomatoes.

Makes 18 muffins, or 4 mini loaves

2 cups (500 mL) buttermilk
6 oz (180 g) butter, melted
2 eggs
2 cups (500 mL) all-purpose flour
2 cups (500 mL) cornmeal
2 tbsp (30 mL) sugar
1 tbsp (15 mL) plus 1 tsp (5 mL) baking powder
1/2 tsp (2 mL) sea salt
1 cup (250 mL) shredded aged cheddar cheese
1/2 lb (250 g) bacon, diced and cooked crisp

Preheat the oven to 450°F (230°C).

In a bowl, mix together the buttermilk, melted butter and eggs. In another bowl, stir together the flour, cornmeal, sugar, baking powder and salt. Stir in the cheese. Toss the bacon into the dry ingredients. Stir the wet ingredients into the dry, mixing just to combine.

Spoon into muffin tins or four 2-cup (500 mL) mini loaf pans. Bake until a toothpick inserted in the centre comes out clean, about 15 minutes for muffins, 20 to 25 minutes for loaves.

Multi-Grain Oat Crackers

Sorry, these are not Raincoast Crisps. Believe me, you're better off letting us make them – they're way too much work! We do love crackers at LSFF, and these tasty morsels are similar in texture to an oatcake, quite mealy and on the drier side. Be sure to bake them thoroughly or else they get stale very quickly. Serve them with smoked salmon, triple cream cheese or aged cheddar.

Makes about 30 crackers

1 3/4 cups (425 mL) all-purpose flour	2 tbsp (30 mL) wheat germ
1 1/4 cups (300 mL) quick oatmeal	1 1/2 tsp (7 mL) sea salt
4 tbsp (60 mL) flaxseed	4 tbsp (60 mL) vegetable oil
4 tbsp (60 mL) old-fashioned rolled oats	2 tbsp (30 mL) olive oil
4 tbsp (60 mL) oat bran	2 tbsp (30 mL) liquid honey
2 tbsp (30 mL) graham cracker crumbs	Coarse sea salt

In a food processor, combine the flour, oatmeal, flaxseed, 4 tbsp (60 mL) rolled oats, oat bran, graham cracker crumbs, wheat germ and salt. Pulse to combine. Add vegetable and olive oils and honey; pulse to combine. Add enough water (about 1/2 cup/125 mL), mixing to make soft, almost moist dough. Let rest for 20 minutes.

Preheat the oven to 325°F (160°C).

Sprinkle parchment paper with more rolled oats and turn out the dough onto the paper. (Depending on the size of the paper, you may need a few sheets and you may need to divide the dough accordingly.) Roll out the dough until very thin; transfer dough and parchment paper to a baking sheet. Sprinkle with coarse salt and score deeply into about 30 squares.

Bake the crackers for 20 to 25 minutes, watching closely after 20 minutes so they don't get too brown (you may want to remove the crackers from edges of pan as they brown). If necessary to dry out excess moisture, reduce heat to low and leave in oven until dry.

Remove from the oven and let cool on pan; gently transfer to a dry container with tight-fitting lid. Crackers can be stored for up to 1 week. If they get soft, just pop them back in a 325°F (160°C) oven for 2 to 3 minutes to freshen.

Grissini

This is adapted from a recipe shown to me by Umberto Menghi's sister Marietta when I was hosting a group at Umberto's villa and cooking school in Tuscany. I noticed that the grissini were always the first thing to vanish from the breadbasket each evening at dinner. Try wrapping a slice of prosciutto around one end of the grissini for a quick hors d'oeuvre.

Makes 3 dozen grissini

1 1/2 cups (375 mL) all-purpose flour
2 tsp (10 mL) active dry yeast
1 tbsp (15 mL) sea salt
2 tsp (10 mL) sugar
2/3 cup (150 mL) water
1/2 cup (125 mL) olive oil
Fine cornmeal

In a mixer with a dough hook, combine the flour, yeast, salt, sugar, water and oil; mix until elastic. Turn out the dough onto a large work surface drizzled with a little olive oil to prevent the dough from sticking. Pat it with your fingers into a large rectangle, about 2 feet (60 cm) long by 6 inches (15 cm) wide. Fold in half lengthwise and press out again to the same size. Fold in half again and press into a rectangle 3 feet (90 cm) by 4 inches (10 cm). Let rest for 20 minutes.

Preheat the oven to 350°F (180°C). Cut the dough into 1-inch (2.5 cm) pieces, then roll each piece into a stick 8 to 10 inches (20 to 25 cm) long, keeping each as close in size as possible. Roll the sticks in the cornmeal to coat and place on a baking sheet. Bake for 15 to 18 minutes. Let cool.

Medici Orrechiette

This dish takes me right back to Italy and the small hilltop village of Radda. I had a version of this pasta dish at a lunch that lasted almost five hours. Service is often slow in Italy. Every bite was worth the wait, as plate after plate of incredible rustic food appeared from the kitchen.

Makes 6 servings

1 lb (500 g) orrechiette
1/4 cup (50 mL) extra-virgin olive oil
3 cloves garlic, crushed
3 tbsp (45 mL) capers, drained
3 tbsp (45 mL) toasted pine nuts
2 tbsp (30 mL) chopped fresh Italian parsley
1 tbsp (15 mL) black olive paste
1 tbsp (15 mL) grated lemon zest
Sea salt and freshly ground pepper
Grated Parmesan cheese

In a large pot of boiling water, cook the orrechiette until al dente. Drain and set aside.

In a large skillet, heat the oil over medium heat; sauté the garlic for 3 to 4 minutes. Add the capers, pine nuts, parsley, olive paste and lemon zest. Reduce heat to low, season to taste with salt and pepper and cook, stirring, over gentle heat for 1 to 2 minutes.

Add the cooked pasta and heat through, stirring, for 2 minutes. Sprinkle with the Parmesan and serve immediately.

Black Bean Linguine with Prawns and Cilantro

This dish may have been the first sign that fusion cuisine had arrived in our kitchen. Salty, spicy and satisfying, it quickly became a simple staple. Try it for a family dinner or save it for a casual meal with friends on the weekend. Bring on the Riesling or Tsingtao beer.

Makes 8 servings

Sea salt
2/3 cup (150 mL) olive oil
3 cloves garlic, minced
3 green onions, chopped
2 jalapeño peppers, seeded and minced
2 lb (1 kg) prawns, peeled, tail intact
6 tbsp (90 mL) oyster sauce
2 tbsp (30 mL) Chinese fermented black beans
1 1/2 tsp (7 mL) sea salt
1 1/2 lb (750 g) linguine
Freshly ground pepper
Fresh cilantro sprigs

In a large pot, bring 4 quarts (4 L) water to a boil; add 2 tsp (10 mL) salt.

Meanwhile, in a skillet, heat the oil over medium-low heat; sauté the garlic, green onions and jalapeño peppers, stirring occasionally, until soft. Add the prawns, oyster sauce, fermented black beans and 1 1/2 tsp (7 mL) salt; sauté for 1 minute. Remove from heat and set aside.

Add the linguine to the pot of boiling water; stir and cook until tender, about 7 minutes for dry pasta, less for fresh. When pasta is almost cooked, return the prawn sauce to heat. Drain pasta; toss with the sauce and season to taste with salt and pepper. Garnish with cilantro and serve immediately.

Extreme Cheese Penne

This rich dish is immoderate comfort food. Ask my stepson, Douglas, who considers it the ultimate mac and cheese – the cheesier the better. (Feel free to experiment with different cheeses: Edam, Asiago, Manchego, Stilton, fontina or pecorino.) Douglas loves to get in the kitchen to cook up a batch, but he's not so thrilled when it comes to the clean-up. Luckily, this doesn't generate too many dirty dishes, which seems to be key when getting teens interested in cooking.

Makes 6 servings

2 3/4 tsp (13 mL) sea salt
1 lb (500 g) penne
5 cups (1.25 L) milk
1/2 cup (125 mL) butter
1/2 cup (125 mL) all-purpose flour
2 1/2 tsp (12 mL) Dijon mustard
1/4 tsp (1 mL) freshly grated nutmeg
1/4 tsp (1 mL) freshly ground pepper
1 1/2 cups (375 mL) shredded aged cheddar cheese
1 cup (250 mL) shredded Swiss or Gruyère cheese
1/2 cup (125 mL) crumbled Cambozola or chèvre
1/3 cup (75 mL) grated Parmesan cheese

Preheat the oven to 350°F (180°C).

Meanwhile, in a large pot, bring 4 quarts (4 L) water to a boil; add 2 tsp (10 mL) of the salt. Add the penne and stir a few times until it comes to the boil. Cook until al dente, 8 to 10 minutes. (It should still have a little resistance when you bite into it.)

In a saucepan, heat the milk over medium-low heat just until warm (do not let come to a boil). In another saucepan, melt the butter; whisk in the flour and let the mixture bubble for a few minutes. Pour in the warm milk, whisking, and cook until the sauce starts to thicken. Add the mustard, nutmeg, remaining salt and pepper; simmer for 3 to 4 minutes. Remove from heat. Stir in the cheddar, Swiss and Cambozola cheeses. Taste and adjust seasoning.

Pour into a 13- x 9-inch (3 L) baking dish. Sprinkle with the Parmesan cheese and bake until golden and bubbling, 30 to 40 minutes. Let stand for 5 minutes before serving.

Seafood Fettuccine with Chili Vodka Cream

This is a dressed-up version of an enormously popular dish we sell in our store: seafood fusilli. Now you can make it at home. Add a salad to start and the equally popular Lemon Almond Dacquoise (page 158) for dessert.

Makes 6 servings

2 tbsp (30 mL) sea salt
1 cup (250 mL) chopped canned tomatoes in heavy purée
1/2 cup (125 mL) vodka
4 tbsp (60 mL) unsalted butter
1 tsp (5 mL) red pepper flakes
1 cup (250 mL) heavy cream
1 lb (500 g) peeled prawns
1 tbsp (15 mL) olive oil
1 lb (500 g) scallops
1 lb (500 g) mussels
1 lb (500 g) dry fettuccine (made with eggs, if possible)
1/2 cup (125 mL) grated Parmesan cheese

In a large pot, bring 5 quarts (5 L) water to a boil. Add salt.

Meanwhile, in a large skillet, combine the tomatoes, vodka, butter and red pepper flakes; bring to a boil and reduce by one-quarter. Stir in the cream and simmer for 15 minutes. Remove from heat and keep warm.

Bring 3 quarts (3 L) water to a boil. Add the prawns and return to a gentle boil. Remove from heat as soon as the prawns turn opaque, about 2 minutes, depending on size. Drain and set aside.

In a sauté pan, heat the oil over medium-high heat; sauté the scallops until just cooked through, 2 to 3 minutes. Set aside.

Place mussels in a dry, heavy saucepan over high heat; cover and cook just until mussels open. Drain. Discard any unopened mussels. Set aside. Add the fettuccine to the pot of boiling water; cook until almost al dente, 3 to 5 minutes. Drain and return to pot; add the seafood and sauce. Heat through, tossing until pasta absorbs some of the sauce, about 1 minute. Transfer to warm serving dishes. Sprinkle with the Parmesan and serve immediately.

Summer Spaghettini with Fresh Corn and Grape Tomatoes

Local tomatoes and corn arrive in the market at the same time and are fabulous in the same dish. Here's one of my favourite late-summer dishes: spaghettini, which is just a thinner version of spaghetti, tossed with tomatoes, corn and basil. What a treat! Go ahead and use any combination of local tomatoes cut into large chunks. We try to indulge in tomatoes as much as we can when they're in season, as it's not long till we're back to the hothouse variety.

Makes 6 servings

1 tsp (5 mL) sea salt
1 cup (250 mL) extra-virgin olive oil
2 cups (500 mL) fresh corn niblets, cut off 4 or 5 cobs
4 cups (1 L) grape or cherry tomatoes, cut in half
1 lb (500 g) spaghettini
2 tsp (10 mL) fresh lemon juice
12 large fresh basil leaves, julienned
Sea salt and freshly ground pepper
1 cup (250 mL) coarsely grated pecorino or Romano cheese

Bring a large pot of water to a boil; add salt.

Meanwhile, in a heavy sauté pan, heat the oil over medium heat; add the corn and heat through. Add the tomatoes; cook until heated through, 2 to 3 minutes. Do not let come to a boil.

Add the spaghettini to the pot of boiling water; cook until al dente, 7 to 8 minutes. Drain and add to the corn mixture; toss to combine. Add the lemon juice, basil, and salt and pepper to taste. Serve warm, passing the cheese to sprinkle on top.

Wild Mushroom Lasagna

Don't curse me halfway through making this. I know it takes a while to make, but oh the compliments you'll get! I actually had a call from someone who had bought our wild mushroom lasagna, taken it to Whistler and eaten it with a group of friends on a hike to the top of a mountain. They just loved it. Now, I wouldn't normally consider lasagna to be picnic food, but maybe I need to change my way of thinking. It's great for the cabin or cottage because once it's assembled, the rest is easy.

Do yourself a favour and double the batch; pop one in the freezer to enjoy another day.

Makes 6 generous servings

1/2 lb (250 g) lasagna noodles

Mushroom Mixture:
3 tbsp (45 mL) olive oil
3 tbsp (45 mL) butter
2 lb (1 kg) button mushrooms, sliced
1 lb (500 g) shiitake mushrooms, sliced
1/2 lb (250 g) fresh wild mushrooms (chanterelle, morel, porcini), sliced
1/4 lb (125 g) shallots, sliced
2 large cloves garlic, crushed

Béchamel Sauce:
1/4 cup (60 mL) butter
1/4 cup (60 mL) all-purpose flour
2 cups (500 mL) milk (use any leftover mushroom juices here
    to top up milk to 2 cups/500 mL)
1/2 cup (125 mL) chopped fresh basil
Sea salt and freshly ground pepper
1 1/2 cups (375 mL) grated Parmesan cheese
Sea salt and freshly ground pepper

Mushroom Mixture: In a large sauté pan, heat 2 tbsp (30 mL) of the oil and all of the butter over medium heat; sauté the button, shiitake and wild mushrooms until browned, 6 to 8 minutes. Drain, reserving juices for béchamel. Remove mushrooms from pan and set aside. In the same pan, heat the remaining oil over medium heat; sauté the shallots and garlic for 3 to 4 minutes. Remove from heat and stir in the mushrooms.

Béchamel Sauce: In a heavy saucepan, melt the butter over low heat. Whisk in the flour and cook, stirring, over very low heat for about 15 minutes. In a saucepan, heat the milk and reserved mushroom juices just until warm. Stir the milk mixture into the flour mixture, whisking to combine.

Stir in the chopped basil. Reserve 1 cup (250 mL) of the béchamel and set aside. Combine the remaining béchamel and mushroom mixture. Season to taste with salt and pepper. Set aside.

Meanwhile, bring a large pot of water to a rolling boil; cook the lasagna noodles until just al dente, 4 to 6 minutes. Drain. Rinse with cold water and spread out on a tea towel.

Preheat the oven to 375°F (190°C). Butter a 13- x 9-inch (3 L) baking dish. Lay 2 lasagna noodles on the bottom of the dish and spread with one-third of the mushroom mixture. Sprinkle with 2 tbsp (30 mL) of the Parmesan. Repeat twice more, ending with pasta noodles. Spread the reserved cup (250 mL) béchamel on top and sprinkle with a generous layer of Parmesan. Cover with buttered foil and bake for 30 minutes. Uncover and bake for 15 minutes more or until bubbling. Let lasagna stand for 15 minutes before serving.

Ricotta Gnocchi with Lemon Spinach Sauce

Along with risotto, good gnocchi is a sure sign of a top restaurant. I can never resist trying it when it's on the menu, although I'm often disappointed – too often gnocchi is heavy and starchy. This recipe is light on the flour and uses more ricotta, which results in a softer, lighter texture, a nice foil to the citrusy sauce.

Makes 6 servings

2 cups (500 mL) ricotta cheese
1/4 cup (50 mL) mascarpone
2 large eggs
1 cup (250 mL) grated Parmesan cheese
Pinch freshly grated nutmeg
Sea salt and freshly ground pepper
1/2 cup (125 mL) plus 2 tbsp (30 mL) all-purpose flour
1/3 cup (75 mL) grated pecorino cheese

Lemon Spinach Sauce:
1 lemon
1 1/2 tbsp (22 mL) butter
1 onion, thinly sliced
1 stalk celery, cut into 1/4-inch (5 mm) thick slices
1/2 cup (125 mL) dry white wine
2 cups (500 mL) heavy cream
1/2 tsp (2 mL) sea salt
1/4 tsp (1 mL) freshly ground pepper
Pinch freshly grated nutmeg
1 cup (250 mL) firmly packed stemmed spinach leaves,
    cut into 1/4-inch (5 mm) strips

Special Equipment:
Pastry bag fitted with 3/4-inch (1.5 cm) plain tip

In a large bowl, use hands to mix together the ricotta and mascarpone until smooth. Beat in the eggs, Parmesan cheese, nutmeg, and salt and pepper to taste until smooth. Gently fold in 1/2 cup (125 mL) of the flour until the dough is the consistency of a stiff mousse.

Sprinkle a baking sheet with the remaining flour. Spoon the dough into a pastry bag fitted with a 3/4-inch (1.5 cm) plain tip. Squeeze out a 1-inch (2.5 cm) cylinder of dough and cut it onto the baking sheet. Repeat with remaining dough. Refrigerate until ready to cook.

Lemon Spinach Sauce: Grate the zest from the lemon and squeeze 2 tbsp (30 mL) of juice. Set aside the zest and juice separately. In a saucepan, melt the butter over medium heat; cook the onion and celery until soft. Add the wine and reserved lemon juice. Bring to a boil and reduce until almost dry, about 10 minutes. Add the cream and boil, reducing until it coats the back of a spoon, 10 to 12 minutes. Strain the sauce through a sieve and season with salt, pepper and nutmeg. Stir in reserved lemon zest. Return to saucepan and set aside.

Preheat the oven to 200°F (100°C).

Meanwhile, in a large pot, bring 4 quarts (4 L) water to a boil; add 1 tbsp (15 mL) salt. Reduce heat and simmer gnocchi until firm, 4 to 5 minutes. Drain and keep warm on a serving platter.

Warm the lemon sauce. Add the spinach and cook, stirring, until wilted. Spoon Lemon Spinach Sauce over gnocchi. Sprinkle with some of the pecorino cheese and pass remaining cheese.

Peking Duck Risotto with Chive Crème Fraîche

A well-made risotto has to be my all-time favourite comfort food. See Lesley's Tips for Perfect Risotto (page 76). The key to a good one is the texture; you want it to be loose when it's finished, not dry and stodgy. The stock must be warm when added to the rice; make sure it's totally absorbed after adding each cupful. Reserve about 1/2 cup (125 mL) to add just before serving, in case the risotto thickens too much. There are so many flavour options that work with risotto: prawn, lemon and crème fraîche; asparagus and scallop; chicken and baby leek.

Makes 6 servings

2 oz (60 g) dried porcini mushrooms
7 cups (1.75 L) chicken stock
6 tbsp (90 mL) extra-virgin olive oil
3 shallots, minced
2 cloves garlic, minced
3/4 lb (375 g) mushrooms
1 Peking duck (purchased from your favourite Chinese butcher)
1 3/4 cups (425 mL) arborio rice
1/2 cup (125 mL) dry white wine
1 cup (250 mL) grated Parmesan cheese
Sea salt and freshly ground pepper

Chive Crème Fraîche:
1/2 cup (125 mL) crème fraîche (page 25)
1 tbsp (15 mL) chopped chives

Chive Crème Fraîche: In a bowl, mix together the crème fraîche and chives. Cover and refrigerate until using.

In a small bowl of warm water, soak the porcini mushrooms until softened, about 20 minutes. In a saucepan, heat the chicken stock over medium heat; keep warm.

In a heavy-bottomed saucepan, heat 2 tbsp (30 mL) of the oil over medium heat; sauté the shallots until translucent. Remove half of the shallots and set aside. Add 3 tbsp (45 mL) more oil to the shallots in the pan; sauté the garlic and mushrooms until soft, about 5 minutes. Set aside.

Remove the breast meat from the Peking duck. Reserve the legs for another use. Remove the skin from the breasts and cut it into thin slivers; set aside. Cut the breast meat finely; add to the mushroom mixture and heat through for 2 to 3 minutes. Remove from heat and set aside.

In a large heavy sauté pan, heat the remaining oil over medium-low heat; add the reserved shallots and rice, stirring to coat rice with oil. Stir in the wine. Stirring continuously, begin to add the warm stock in 1-cup (250 mL) increments, allowing rice to absorb all the liquid before the next addition. After 6 cups (1.5 L), slow down the addition to 1/2 cup (125 mL) at a time and begin tasting the rice for doneness. Just before al dente, remove from heat and gently mix in the reserved duck meat mixture and reserved skin. Slowly stir in the cheese. This will thicken the risotto, so it needs to be served immediately. Season to taste with salt and pepper and ladle into bowls. Top each serving with a spoonful of Chive Crème Fraîche.

Lesley's Tips for Perfect Risotto

**Risotto is a rice dish cooked in the traditional northern Italian way.
For best results, follow these guidelines.**

1. Use a large saucepan and do not cover. A wide pot is best, to contain the rice in as thin a layer as possible, allowing for even absorption of the stock.

2. Risotto should be made at the last minute and served immediately. It takes about 20 minutes to cook, so plan ahead.

3. The key to great risotto is the rice itself. Use medium-grain. The first choice is Italian *superfino*, such as arborio, roma, vialone or carnaroli. A medium grain releases starch as it cooks, creating a creamy, rich texture. You can use other grains, such as barley, for an interesting variation, but choose one that will retain its texture. Just remember that if you're making risotto without rice, the creaminess will need to come from adding butter or cheese.

4. Use a mild-flavoured stock so as not to overwhelm the subtle flavour of risotto. Add the simmering stock slowly and stir constantly. So that the grains do not dry out, burn or stick, use a wooden spoon with a flat edge to scrape the entire bottom of the pan when stirring. Stirring constantly will create an evenly cooked risotto.

5. Aim for a creamy consistency with an al dente bite. During cooking, the rice absorbs the stock and slowly cooks from the outside in. Just before the nucleus of the grain is cooked, the rice is done and must be removed from the heat. The grain should have just a suggestion of resistance when you bite into it.

6. If the risotto is too thick, just before serving you can adjust by adding a little more stock. Risotto should not be stodgy.

7. If adding purées for flavouring or other quick-cooking flavouring ingredients (asparagus, corn, finely diced tomato, cheese), add them near the end so you don't lose their texture, colour or flavour, and so you don't adversely affect the texture of the risotto.

8. Stir the risotto vigorously at the end of cooking. Stirring in lots of butter and cheese makes it the ultimate comfort food. That's how they do it in the authentic northern Italian manner.

9. Don't throw away any leftovers in the pot. Make risotto cakes with the chilled rice. Scoop cold risotto – an ice cream scoop works very well – into a ball and flatten it to about 1/2" (1 cm) thick to form a cake. Saute in 1/2 tsp (2 mL) of butter and 1/2 tsp (2 mL) of olive oil for each cake for about 10 to 12 minutes, or until golden on both sides.

Parmesan Polenta with Baby Leeks

Polenta is to the northern Italians as rice is to the Chinese – a staple of their diet. This cornmeal dish shows up in many variations, from this creamy, soft version to crispy fried triangles topped with antipasti.

Makes 6 servings

4 1/2 cups (1.125 L) water
1 1/2 tsp (7 mL) sea salt
1 cup (250 mL) stone-ground yellow cornmeal
1/2 cup (125 mL) light cream
2 tbsp (30 mL) butter
1/3 cup (75 mL) grated Parmesan cheese
Freshly ground pepper
2 tsp (10 mL) finely chopped chives

Leek Mixture:
2 tsp (10 mL) olive oil
2 baby leeks (white part only), coarsely chopped
1 clove garlic, minced
1/2 stalk celery, finely chopped

Leek Mixture: In a heavy sauté pan, heat the oil over medium-low heat; gently cook leeks, garlic and celery, stirring, until soft and just slightly golden, 10 to 15 minutes. Set aside.

Place a serving dish in the oven to warm. In a saucepan over high heat, combine the water and salt and bring to a boil. Gradually pour in the cornmeal, whisking constantly. When the mixture begins to bubble, reduce heat to medium-low and cook, stirring, until the cornmeal begins to thicken, 20 to 30 minutes. Slowly whisk in the leek mixture. Add the cream, butter and half of the Parmesan cheese. Pour into the warmed serving dish and sprinkle with the remaining Parmesan cheese, pepper and chives. Serve immediately.

Wild Rice, Lentils and Pearl Barley with Toasted Pine Nuts

Here's a dish so versatile that it can serve as a delicious side dish for a family dinner or be multiplied to feed a crowd. Or add strips of grilled chicken and papaya for an interesting luncheon dish. Do experiment with the grains; try substituting orzo for the bulgur and quinoa for the pearl barley for a different combination of flavours and textures.

Makes 6 servings

1/4 cup (50 mL) olive oil
3 cloves garlic, crushed
1 red onion, chopped
5 green onions, chopped
1/4 cup (50 mL) wild rice
4 cups (1 L) chicken stock
1/2 tsp (2 mL) dried oregano
1/2 cup (125 mL) pearl barley
1/2 cup (125 mL) lentils, rinsed and drained
1/4 cup (50 mL) bulgur
1/2 cup (125 mL) pine nuts, toasted
1/4 cup (50 mL) packed finely chopped fresh parsley
Sea salt and freshly ground pepper

In a heavy 4-quart (4 L) saucepan, heat the oil over medium-low heat; sauté the garlic, onion and green onions until softened, about 5 minutes. Stir in the wild rice along with 2 cups (500 mL) of stock and oregano; bring to a boil. Reduce heat, cover and simmer for 30 minutes. Add the barley and another cup (250 mL) of the stock; simmer for 15 minutes.

Add the lentils and bulgur to the pan. Pour in the remaining stock and bring to a boil. Reduce heat, cover and simmer until grains are tender, about 30 minutes. Uncover and simmer until any remaining liquid evaporates. Stir in the pine nuts and parsley. Season to taste with salt and pepper.

Catering Adventures

Can you imagine inviting 50 people for drinks and a light supper, only to have your oven break down 30 minutes before the guests arrive? This is the sort of adventure LSFF would encounter regularly; being the magicians we were, we found a way to work through whatever situation arose. Thank goodness for gas barbecues! Have you ever tried to cook chicken potpie on a barbecue?

One of my favourite escapades was the evening we catered a dinner for 60 guests at a private home. Somehow, on the way to the party, one of the staff members got lost. This was back in the days before cellphones were as common as wallets. After an hour into set-up, with no server in sight, I got on the phone to my mother and asked her to help. Luckily for me, my mother is a real sport. She arrived in no time, threw on a uniform and did a fantastic job. Unfortunately, my father wasn't as keen as I was about keeping her on the payroll. Come to think of it, my father is the only member of the family who hasn't donned an apron at some point. My brother and several cousins have cheerfully tended bar, and my sister, numerous cousins and children of friends have served and cooked at parties, parked cars, set tables and bussed trays and trays of glasses.

Chapter Four

MAINS: MEAT & POULTRY

At dinnertime, meat is often the main event. It sets the mood, be it a rich braise of beef or a spicy summer chicken on the barbecue.

Although beef played a minor role in our storefront menu, it was always a favourite at catered events. On a daily basis, I think our clients preferred to eat chicken or fish and maybe throw a steak on the barbecue themselves. When we did offer beef, it was either braised or stewed; generally, unless beef is in this form it doesn't reheat well. In the winter months, nothing can beat braised short ribs with Parmesan polenta, risotto or mashed potatoes. Pair it with a good bottle of Shiraz and you have a comfort food dinner made in heaven.

Chicken, on the other hand, has to be one of the most versatile and loved main-course ingredients. I could devote a whole book to chicken recipes because – like shoes – you can never have too many. I'm quite adamant about using free-range birds because there's absolutely no comparison in taste or texture between a mass-produced chicken and a free-range, unmedicated one. I urge you whenever possible to buy free-range. If you can only find the whole bird, either ask your butcher to cut it up for you or try doing it yourself. It's really quite simple: remove the leg and thigh first, then cut through the centre of the breasts and cut through each side of the back.

The variety of cooking methods for chicken ranges from grilling and roasting to braising and broiling. It's great marinated and served hot or cold, and is suitable for everything from a casual barbecue get-together to a formal event. I've given you a few dishes that have been very popular in our store and at catered parties. The Chicken Breasts Stuffed with Muffuletta and Chèvre are so easy to make but can be served at your smartest dinner party. There are endless variations on this dish; for example, replace the chèvre with Boursin or Cambozola or brie. Instead of using muffuletta, tuck in some sautéed mushrooms, artichoke hearts, prosciutto or cooked wild rice. You could entertain for weeks with just this one recipe. The Barbecued Thai Chicken is also perfect for a crowd because you can easily multiply it and keep a batch of the sauce in your fridge or freezer for spontaneous entertaining.

Veal Chops with Sun-Dried Tomato and Basil

A number of years ago, a friend who was in the pink veal business – where calves are pasture-raised, versus milk-fed – asked me to develop some recipes. This was one of the favourites. You can easily substitute chicken breasts if you prefer.

Makes 6 servings

3 tbsp (45 mL) olive oil
12 small shallots, halved lengthwise
Sea salt and freshly ground pepper
2 cups (500 mL) chicken stock
1/3 cup (75 mL) pine nuts, lightly toasted
1/4 cup (50 mL) dry white wine
8 oil-packed sun-dried tomatoes, drained and cut into matchstick strips
6 veal chops (each 6 oz/180 g)
1/2 cup (125 mL) cold unsalted butter, cubed
1 tbsp (15 mL) chopped fresh basil

Preheat the oven to 325°F (160°C).

In a shallow baking pan, combine the oil, shallots, and salt and pepper to taste, stirring to coat shallots. Roast until brown and soft, about 30 minutes. In a saucepan over medium heat, reduce chicken stock to 1/2 cup (125 mL).

In a skillet over medium heat, cook the roasted shallots, pine nuts, wine and sun-dried tomatoes until the wine is nearly evaporated. Set aside.

Grease the barbecue and preheat to medium-high.

Season the veal chops with salt and pepper and place on the grill; cook for 5 minutes. Reduce heat to medium and turn chops; cook until medium-rare, 6 to 7 minutes. Remove from heat and set aside.

Add the reduced stock to the shallot mixture; simmer until reduced and thickened to consistency of sauce. Whisk in the butter a bit at a time. Spoon sauce over veal and sprinkle basil on top. Serve immediately.

Beef Tenderloin with Double-Smoked Bacon and Porcini Mushrooms

This is one of our favourite pull-out-all-the-stops party dishes. When guests are coming or you're hosting a special family occasion, this dish is just the thing. Porcini mushrooms have an earthy, woodsy flavour, so pair them with bacon for a rich, satisfying dish that's chic at the same time.

Makes 6 to 8 servings

1 cup (250 mL) dried porcini mushrooms
1 beef tenderloin, 3 to 4 lb (1.5 to 2 kg)
Sea salt and freshly ground pepper
6 tbsp (90 mL) olive oil
5 strips double-smoked bacon, cut into 1/4-inch (5 mm) pieces
1 cup (250 mL) shallots, sliced
4 cloves garlic, sliced
1/2 sprig fresh rosemary
4 cups (1 L) dark veal stock
1 cup (250 mL) port
2 tbsp (30 mL) cold butter

Preheat the oven to 375°F (190°C).

In a bowl, pour 1 cup (250 mL) boiling water over the porcini mushrooms; let stand until softened, about 20 minutes.

Remove the thin membrane and any fat on the outside of the tenderloin. Season the meat with salt and pepper. In a heavy skillet, heat 3 tbsp (45 mL) of the oil over medium-high heat; brown the tenderloin on all sides for about 1 minute per side. Transfer to a roasting pan. Pour off the fat from the skillet.

In the same skillet, cook the bacon until almost crisp; remove from pan and set aside. Drain off the bacon fat and discard.

Drain the mushrooms, reserving the soaking liquid. In the same skillet, heat 2 tbsp (30 mL) of the remaining oil over medium heat; sauté the mushrooms until soft and golden. Remove from pan; season with salt and pepper and set aside.

Add the remaining oil to the pan; sauté the shallots, garlic and rosemary until shallots are soft, 3 to 4 minutes. Add the bacon, veal stock and port. Simmer over medium heat until liquid is reduced by half. Set aside.

Roast the tenderloin in the oven for 15 to 20 minutes. Transfer the meat to a cutting board, reserving the liquid in pan. Place the pan over medium-high heat and simmer until reduced by one-third. Whisk in the cold butter, a bit at a time, until smooth. Add the mushrooms and stir gently.

Slice the tenderloin and arrange on warm plates. Spoon the mushroom sauce over top and serve immediately.

Balsamic Short Ribs with Sautéed Spinach

I recommend doubling this recipe and freezing what you don't need.

This is so good, it could become your Sunday special in the winter. A braising dish cannot be hurried, so make sure you allow enough time for the ribs to simmer gently. Serve it with Wild Rice, Lentils and Pearl Barley with Toasted Pine Nuts (page 78) or with simple mashed potatoes. Have your butcher cut the ribs to the right length if they're too long.

Makes 6 servings

3 lb (1.5 kg) beef short ribs, in 1 3/4-inch (4 cm) lengths
Sea salt and freshly ground white pepper
4 tbsp (60 mL) olive oil
1 cup (250 mL) coarsely chopped onions
6 cloves garlic, crushed
1 cup (250 mL) coarsely chopped carrots
2 cups (500 mL) dry red wine
1 cup (250 mL) balsamic vinegar
4 cups (1 L) beef stock
4 sprigs fresh thyme
1 bay leaf
1 lb (500 g) fresh spinach
Freshly grated nutmeg

Preheat the oven to 350°F (180°C).

Trim off and discard excess fat from the short ribs. Sprinkle both sides with salt and white pepper.

Divide half of the oil between 2 large skillets and heat over medium-high heat. Divide the ribs between the 2 pans (or sear them in batches in one pan) and sear until brown on all sides, 5 to 7 minutes. Transfer to a platter and set aside.

Pour off all but 1 tbsp (15 mL) fat from one of the pans and decrease heat to medium; cook the onions, garlic and carrots until caramelized and golden brown, about 4 minutes. Remove from pan. Add the wine and balsamic vinegar to the pan and deglaze, stirring to release the caramelized bits on the bottom of the pan.

Pour the wine mixture and the stock into a large roasting pan; add the ribs, caramelized onion mixture, thyme and bay leaf. Cover and roast in the oven until meat is very tender, 3 to 4 hours.

Remove ribs, reserving liquid, and keep warm in low oven. In a large shallow saucepan over medium-high heat, reduce the reserved liquid until it coats the back of a spoon, 15 to 20 minutes.

In a large sauté pan, heat the remaining oil over medium-high heat; add the spinach and cook, stirring constantly, until wilted, about 2 minutes. Season to taste with nutmeg, salt and pepper. Spoon some of the sauce over each serving of short ribs and top with sautéed spinach.

Grilled Balsamic Lime Flank Steak with Endive, Romaine and Watercress Salad and Basil Pecan Vinaigrette

Flank steak is an underrated cut of meat. It's so easy to prepare and garners reams of compliments when prepared properly. You want to cook it until medium-rare and let it rest for 10 minutes before slicing. The lime juice and balsamic vinegar tenderize and flavour the meat.

Makes 8 servings

2/3 cup (150 mL) balsamic vinegar
1/4 cup (50 mL) extra-virgin olive oil
1/4 cup (50 mL) fresh lime juice
2 tsp (10 mL) crushed garlic
Sea salt and freshly ground pepper
1 flank steak, about 2 1/2 lb (1.25 kg)

Salad:
1 head romaine
2 Belgian endives, halved then julienned
1 bunch watercress, stems removed

Basil Pecan Vinaigrette:
1/3 cup (75 mL) red wine vinegar
1/4 cup (50 mL) coarsely chopped fresh basil
1 tbsp (15 mL) prepared Dijon mustard
1 cup (250 mL) extra-virgin olive oil
1/2 cup (125 mL) finely ground pecans
Sea salt and freshly ground pepper

Salad: Wash and dry the romaine; tear into pieces. In a salad bowl, mix together the romaine, endives and watercress. Set aside in refrigerator until ready to use.

In shallow baking dish or plastic bag, combine the balsamic vinegar, oil, lime juice, garlic, and salt and pepper to taste. Add flank steak and marinate in refrigerator for 1/2 to 2 hours.

Preheat the barbecue to medium-high. Remove the steak from the marinade, discarding marinade. Place on the grill and cook until medium-rare, 5 to 6 minutes per side (any longer and steak will be tough as a boot!). Transfer to a cutting board and let rest for 10 minutes before slicing thinly across the grain.

Basil Pecan Vinaigrette: Whisk together the vinegar, basil and mustard. Slowly whisk in the oil until mixture emulsifies and comes together. Gently fold in the pecans. Season to taste with salt and pepper. Refrigerate only if necessary; dressing should be served at room temperature. Drizzle over salad and toss just before serving.

Place a few slices of steak on each plate and arrange a portion of dressed salad alongside.

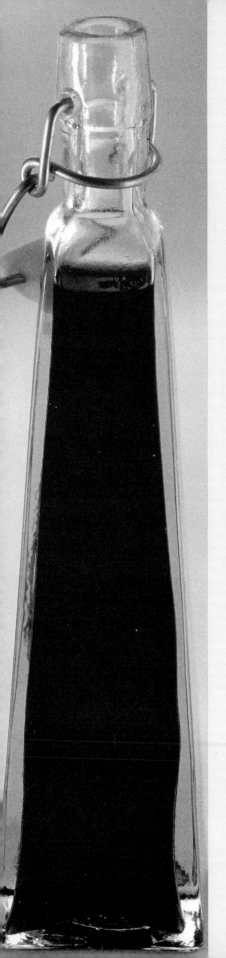

Balsamic Vinegar

Balsamico is the darling of the vinegar world. In North America, balsamic vinegar sprang onto the culinary map at the beginning of the 1980s, and suddenly it was almost as though we ourselves had discovered it. In truth, balsamic vinegar has been produced in Italy since the 11th century, at which time only the nobility and the very wealthy were able to enjoy it. Italian dukes used to carry flasks of it to ward off everything from the plague to indigestion.

Actually, most of the balsamic vinegar that arrives here from Italy is not what the Italians consider true balsamic vinegar. The real, or traditionally made, kind comes from the cities Modena and Reggio, where strict regulations control the process, right down to the labelling and type of bottle used.

The process of making balsamic starts with the grapes – traditionally Trebbiano grapes, picked late in the season when their sugar content is greatest. The grapes are set out in boxes to dry slightly, concentrating the juices. The juice is then pressed out, and the must is cooked in large open vats. During this process, the sugars caramelize slightly, creating one of the flavour elements essential to the final product. Next, the syrup is stored in the first of a series of barrels, allowing it to pick up flavours from the wood. Each barrel is a different type of wood, ranging from mulberry to cherry. A minimum of three and a maximum of five barrels might be used. Vinegar must be aged for a minimum of 12 years before it can be submitted to a consortium for evaluation. If approved, it's decanted into the appropriate bottles and labelled with either a gold, silver or red seal – gold being the top grade – before being returned to the producer. This long, involved process is why true balsamic vinegar is so expensive.

So what are we buying most of the time when we pick up balsamic vinegar at the grocery store? There are as many grades and qualities out there as there are brands, the lowest being industrial-grade balsamic made from basic vinegar that has sugar and caramel flavour added to it. It's often harsh and quite nasty. In the top grades, wine must and aged wine vinegar are blended to produce a lovely balsamic condiment perfect for salad dressings, sauces and marinades. So buyer, beware: you usually get what you pay for when it comes to balsamic. Look for a rich, deep amber colour with some viscosity and a flavour that's sweet and tart, with woodsy cherry characteristics.

Try sprinkling balsamic vinegar over roasted new potatoes as a substitute for butter. Or simmer the vinegar until it's reduced to half the volume (this will give it more body and intensify the flavour) and drizzle it over grilled vegetables or meat. You can also stir it into tomato sauce to add some punch. For a real twist, mix it with honey to serve with berries and ice cream.

Grilled Beef Ribs with Sweet Dark Barbecue Sauce

Pork ribs always seem to take centre stage when it comes to barbecuing ribs in the summer, but beef ribs are more substantial and satisfy the meat eaters in the family.

Makes 6 to 8 servings

6 lb (3 kg) beef ribs
2 stalks celery, cut into 4-inch (10 cm) lengths
3 carrots, cut into 4-inch (10 cm) lengths
1 small onion, quartered
1 bay leaf
6 black peppercorns
Sweet Dark Barbecue Sauce (recipe follows)

In a large stockpot or Dutch oven, combine the ribs, celery, carrots, onion, bay leaf and black peppercorns. Cover the ribs with cold water and place over medium heat. Simmer for 2 hours. Drain ribs; discard the veggies, bay leaf and peppercorns. The ribs can be cooled, covered and refrigerated, overnight.

Preheat the barbecue to medium-low or preheat the oven to 300°F (150°C). Brush as much Sweet Dark Barbecue Sauce as you like over the ribs and grill or roast, turning and basting occasionally, for about 1 hour.

Sweet Dark Barbecue Sauce

This barbecue sauce recipe yields 4 cups (1 L), so you're going to have extra. You'll use about half the sauce for the ribs, so place the remainder in a covered container in the fridge for future use. It will keep refrigerated for at least four weeks – handy for brushing on chicken breasts or pork chops. Just don't put your basting brush into the container of extra sauce; pour out what you might need in advance.

Makes 4 cups (1 L)

4 cups (1 L) ketchup
2/3 cup (150 mL) white vinegar
1/3 cup (75 mL) Dijon mustard
1 tbsp (15 mL) fresh lemon juice
1 1/4 cups (300 mL) packed brown sugar
1/4 onion, minced
1 tbsp (15 mL) celery seed
1 tbsp (15 mL) minced garlic
1 tbsp (15 mL) freshly ground pepper
1 tbsp (15 mL) ground cumin
1/3 cup (75 mL) butter

In a bowl, combine the ketchup, vinegar, mustard, lemon juice, sugar, onion, celery seed, garlic, pepper and cumin; bring to a boil and simmer for 1 hour. Remove from heat and whisk in butter.

Butterflied Leg of Lamb
with Citrus Tapenade and White Bean Purée

Ask your butcher to bone the leg of lamb for you. A butterflied leg of lamb is easier to cook and you'll get more consistent results. Be sure the meat is at room temperature before grilling.

Makes 6 to 8 servings

1 leg of lamb, butterflied
2 to 3 tbsp (30 to 45 mL) chopped fresh thyme
1/4 cup (50 mL) chopped fresh mint
2 cloves garlic, crushed
1/2 tsp (2 mL) sea salt and freshly ground pepper
Extra-virgin olive oil
Citrus Tapenade (recipe follows)
White Bean Purée (recipe follows)

Trim excess fat off the leg of lamb (this is important as lamb fat has a tendency to cause flare-ups). Crush together the thyme, mint, garlic, salt and pepper; smear over all sides of the lamb. Let marinate for 1 hour at room temperature, or overnight in the refrigerator (if the latter, let come to room temperature before continuing).

Preheat the grill to medium-high.

Lightly brush the lamb with olive oil. Place on the grill, close lid and cook until medium-rare, about 15 minutes per side. Serve with Citrus Tapenade and White Bean Purée on the side.

This tapenade is very versatile. Not only is it a delicious addition to the lamb but it's also fabulous served with goat cheese and crackers, as a topping for pizza or tossed on warm linguine for a simple dinner.

Citrus Tapenade

Makes 1 cup (250 mL)

1 cup (250 mL) kalamata or niçoise olives
3 tbsp (45 mL) extra-virgin olive oil
1 1/2 tbsp (22 mL) chopped fresh parsley
1 tbsp (15 mL) chopped fresh mint
2 tsp (10 mL) grated orange zest
2 tsp (10 mL) grated lemon zest
1 tbsp (15 mL) fresh lemon juice
Sea salt and freshly ground pepper

Pit and coarsely chop the olives. Place in a bowl along with the oil, parsley, mint, orange zest, lemon zest and lemon juice. Season to taste with salt and pepper if necessary. Let stand at room temperature until serving.

In France, pairing lamb with white beans is a classic combination. Beans are a welcome change from potatoes.

White Bean Purée

Makes 6 to 8 servings

4 tbsp (60 mL) olive oil
2 small onions, thinly sliced
6 cloves garlic, thinly sliced
1 tsp (5 mL) ground cumin
5 cups (1.25 L) cooked cannellini beans

2 1/2 cups (625 mL) water
2 bay leaves
1 tsp (5 mL) finely chopped fresh rosemary
6 tbsp (90 mL) fresh lemon juice
3 to 4 tsp (15 to 20 mL) sea salt

In a saucepan, heat half of the oil over medium-high heat; sauté the onions for 5 minutes. Add the garlic and cumin; cook until onions are soft, about 5 minutes. Add the beans, water, bay leaves and rosemary; cook for 5 minutes longer. Reduce heat to low and cook until the beans are very soft and the mixture is thick, 15 to 20 minutes. Remove from heat and discard the bay leaves. Add the remaining oil and lemon juice. Transfer to a food processor and purée until smooth. Season to taste with salt. Press through a fine-mesh sieve. Discard any remaining solids.

To serve, reheat in a saucepan over low heat until warmed through. Serve immediately with the lamb.

Slow-Braised Rabbit in White Port, Prunes and Green Olives

This recipe reminds me of my year in France, where rabbit is almost as popular as chicken. Because rabbit is so lean, braising is the best method of cooking it. Try this in the fall when the weather is just starting to turn to sweater season. Serve it with the Tuscan Potato Cakes (page 133). Order the rabbit from your butcher or, if you wish, you can substitute 12 chicken thighs for the rabbit.

Makes 6 to 8 servings

2 whole rabbits
2 tbsp (30 mL) fresh lemon juice
1 1/2 tbsp (22 mL) minced garlic
2 tsp (10 mL) cinnamon
2 tbsp (30 mL) olive oil
2 tbsp (30 mL) butter
24 pitted prunes
2 cups (500 mL) white port
24 pearl onions
2/3 cup (150 mL) chicken stock
1 tsp (5 mL) grated orange zest
1/4 cup (50 mL) freshly squeezed orange juice
Sea salt and freshly ground pepper
24 green olives

Cut rabbit into 9 pieces: start by removing each of the legs, cutting through the joints; cut the back legs into thigh and leg; then cut the saddle (or body) into 3 pieces.

In a mortar and pestle or food processor, grind together the lemon juice, garlic and 1 3/4 tsp (8 mL) of the cinnamon to make a paste; rub over the rabbit pieces. In a sauté pan or shallow casserole over medium heat, heat the oil and butter; brown the rabbit pieces on all sides. Place in a Dutch oven.

In a small saucepan over medium-high heat, combine the prunes and 1/2 cup (125 mL) of the port; simmer for 5 minutes. Remove from heat and let stand until plump, about 10 minutes. Drain, discarding liquid; set prunes aside.

Meanwhile, peel the onions and trim the root ends carefully, leaving the ends intact. Cut an X in each root end so that the insides of the onions don't telescope or pop out when cooked. In a large pot of salted water over medium heat, simmer the onions until tender but not mushy, 5 to 7 minutes. Drain. (If you want a richer dish, sauté the onions in 3 tbsp/45 mL butter and 2 tbsp/30 mL sugar until glazed and rich brown.)

In a small saucepan over medium-high heat, combine the remaining port, stock, orange zest and juice and remaining cinnamon; bring to a simmer. Pour over rabbit pieces in pan; place pan over medium-low heat, cover and simmer until rabbit is tender, about 25 minutes. Reserving sauce in pan, remove the rabbit pieces, cover and keep warm.

Reduce the reserved sauce over medium heat until slightly thickened, about 5 minutes. Season to taste with salt and pepper. Add prunes, onions and olives; return to a simmer and heat through. Arrange rabbit on plates and spoon prune sauce over top.

G.L. Lamb Burgers
with Feta Mayonnaise and Mint

This is my husband's (G.L. are his initials) surefire method to impress anyone who likes lamb. If you haven't tried a lamb burger, you're in for a treat and will be hard pressed to go back to beef burgers. The secret is that ground lamb has a fair amount of fat, and that's always the key to juicy burgers. These days, everyone buys extra-lean ground beef, but unfortunately fat equals flavour, and an extra-lean burger tends to be dry when cooked through. Lamb burgers, when cooked properly, always stay juicy and flavourful. Combine them with chewy buns, sheep's milk feta and good-quality mint jelly and you'll definitely have your money's worth out of this cookbook.

Makes 6 servings

2 1/2 lb (1.25 kg) ground lamb
Sea salt and freshly ground pepper
6 good-quality crusty hamburger rolls
5 oz (150 g) feta cheese (preferably sheep's milk)
1/2 cup (125 mL) mayonnaise
1/3 cup (75 mL) mint jelly (preferably Burgess or Scotts;
    no bright green jelly)

Preheat the barbecue to medium-low.

Using your hands, gently mix the lamb with salt and pepper to taste. Form into 6 patties (the patties may seem very generous, but the meat will shrink a lot during cooking). Place on the grill and cook until juices run clear, 5 to 6 minutes per side, depending on thickness.

Slice the rolls in half; toast rolls, cut side down, on the grill just until slightly brown, 1 to 2 minutes.

In a small bowl, blend the feta with the mayonnaise. While meat is still warm, slather with the feta mixture. Spread a generous amount of mint jelly on each toasted roll; place the burgers in the rolls and serve.

Chicken Breast Stuffed with Spinach, Pine Nuts and Pancetta

Variations of this dish have been on our menu for years, but I always come back to the original as a reliable party dish. Multiply the recipe and you can happily feed a crowd. The dish can be made in advance, reheats well and stays moist and delicious. It's also good served cold with a salad the next day.

Makes 6 servings

1 tbsp (15 mL) olive oil (plus extra for brushing)
1/2 small white onion, minced
1 tsp (5 mL) minced garlic
6 thin slices pancetta, diced
3 cups (750 mL) chopped fresh spinach
1 tbsp (15 mL) chopped fresh rosemary
1/3 cup (75 mL) grated Parmesan cheese
1/3 cup (75 mL) toasted pine nuts, chopped
6 boneless chicken breasts, skin on
Sea salt and freshly ground pepper

In a skillet, heat 1 tbsp (15 mL) oil over medium heat; sauté the onion, garlic and pancetta until pancetta is slightly crispy. Add the spinach and rosemary and toss well to combine; cook, tossing, until spinach is just wilted. Remove from heat and let cool; mix in Parmesan and pine nuts.

Preheat the oven to 375°F (190°C).

Run your fingers between the skin of the chicken and the meat to create a pocket. Stuff the pancetta mixture evenly under the skin. Brush lightly with oil and season to taste with salt and pepper. Bake until chicken is cooked through and juices run clear when pierced, 20 to 30 minutes. Serve warm.

Chicken Breasts Stuffed with Muffuletta and Chèvre

Muffuletta is a mixture of olives, artichoke hearts, capers, sun-dried tomatoes and olive oil. You can buy prepared muffuletta or use our recipe on page 8. This dish can be served warm or cold. It's great to make in warm weather and enjoy cold with a salad for a light dinner or to pack up for the beach along with Grilled Tuscan Vegetables (page 125).

Makes 6 servings

1 cup (250 mL) Muffuletta (page 8)
1/2 cup (125 mL) crumbled chèvre
6 boneless chicken breasts, skin on
Olive oil
Sea salt and freshly ground pepper

Preheat the oven to 375°F (190°C).

In a bowl, mix the Muffuletta with the chèvre. Run your fingers between the skin and the meat of the chicken breast to create a pocket. Stuff the Muffuletta mixture evenly under the skin. Brush skin with oil. Place on a baking sheet and sprinkle with salt and pepper. Bake until chicken is cooked through and juices run clear when pierced, 20 to 30 minutes.

Making Stock from Scratch

Here's an easy method for making dark, rich chicken stock. You can use any quantity of chicken you have available. Add the veggies as you like, depending on your flavour preferences.

Chicken bones
Onion, unpeeled and quartered
Celery
Carrots
Bay leaf
Thyme
Parsley
Black peppercorns

In a roasting pan, combine the chicken bones, onion quarters, celery and carrots; roast in a 350°F (180°C) oven until dark caramel brown. Transfer the mixture to a stockpot; pour in enough cold water to cover. Add the bay leaf, thyme, parsley and black peppercorns. Bring to a boil; reduce heat and simmer for 2 hours. Strain and discard the solids. Return the strained stock to the pot and simmer over medium heat until liquid is reduced by half. Let cool in fridge. Skim off any fat solids from the top before using.

Roasted Breast of Chicken with Garlic and Candied Lemon

If you're looking for a sophisticated little chicken dish, this is it. The key here is to make deeply coloured, deeply flavoured stock. There's a lot of garlic in this dish, but it's cooked long enough to make it soft and sweet – a perfect contrast to the candied lemon zest.

Makes 6 servings

4 lemons
3 tbsp (45 mL) sugar
1/2 cup (125 mL) water
1/4 cup (50 mL) olive oil
2 heads garlic, separated into cloves and peeled
6 single free-range chicken breasts
2 cups (500 mL) rich dark chicken stock
    (see Making Stock from Scratch, page 99)
Sea salt and freshly ground pepper

Using a vegetable peeler, remove the peel, but not the white pith, from the lemons. Cut into thin strips and place in a saucepan along with the sugar and water. Bring to a simmer and cook until the peel is translucent, 10 to 15 minutes. Strain and let cool. Juice the lemons and set aside.

Preheat the oven to 425°F (220°C).

In a heavy, ovenproof sauté pan, heat the oil over medium heat; add the garlic cloves and chicken breasts. Brown chicken on both sides. Add the chicken stock and lemon juice. Bring to a boil over high heat on stovetop, then roast in the oven for about 15 minutes, or until chicken is golden and juices run clear when pierced. Reserving sauce in pan, transfer chicken to a warm serving platter and cover with foil to keep warm.

Reduce the sauce until it coats the back of a spoon, 20 to 30 minutes. Add the candied lemon. Season to taste with salt and pepper and spoon the sauce over the chicken breasts to serve.

Braised Chicken with Pancetta and Oven-Roasted Tomatoes

Braising goes hand in hand with cooler temperatures. There's something very comforting about having a pot on the stove or in the oven simmering away when the wind is howling outside. Try this dish with the Parmesan Polenta with Baby Leeks (page 77) or Chèvre Mashed Potatoes (page 136) to sop up all the delicious sauce. This recipe needs to be started the night before, as the tomatoes must roast overnight.

Makes 6 servings

2 tbsp (30 mL) olive oil
12 bone-in chicken thighs, skin on
10 slices pancetta, julienned
1 onion, diced
2 tsp (10 mL) minced garlic
1 cup (250 mL) white wine
2 cups (500 mL) chicken stock
1 tbsp (15 mL) chopped fresh rosemary
10 pieces Oven-Roasted Tomatoes (recipe below)
2 tbsp (30 mL) chopped fresh Italian parsley

Oven-Roasted Tomatoes:
4 roma tomatoes
1 tsp (5 mL) fennel seeds
1/2 tsp (2 mL) sea salt
1/4 tsp (1 mL) freshly ground pepper

Oven-Roasted Tomatoes: Preheat the oven to lowest temperature setting. Quarter the tomatoes; toss with fennel seeds, salt and pepper. Arrange in a single layer on a baking sheet and roast overnight.

Preheat the oven to 375°F (190°C).

In a heavy, ovenproof sauté pan, heat the oil over medium-high heat; sear the chicken thighs until slightly golden, about 2 minutes per side. Remove chicken and set aside. In the same pan, sauté the pancetta until crisp. Add the onion, garlic and wine, stirring to deglaze. Stir in the stock and rosemary. Return chicken to pan; cover and place in oven. Braise for 45 to 60 minutes, or until juices run clear when chicken is pierced. Remove the chicken, reserving liquid, and place on a platter.

If necessary, reduce the cooking liquid over medium-high heat to thicken slightly. Add the tomatoes and parsley; heat through, stirring. Pour over chicken. Serve warm.

Parmesan-Crusted Chicken

Parmesan and oatmeal? It may sound like an odd combination, but it's all about the texture. Every summer, we try to come up with new chicken recipes that work well as picnic food, without going the deep-fried route. This chicken has a great crust, stays moist, and can be served on its own or with pesto mayonnaise on the side.

Makes 6 servings

1 egg
3/4 cup (175 mL) all-purpose flour
1 tsp (5 mL) sea salt
1/4 tsp (1 mL) freshly ground pepper
3/4 cup (175 mL) grated Parmesan cheese
1 1/2 cups (375 mL) oatmeal
3 tbsp (45 mL) chopped fresh basil or herbes de Provence
6 boneless skinless chicken breasts
1/2 cup (125 mL) butter, melted

Preheat the oven to 375°F (190°C). Line a baking sheet with parchment paper or oil lightly.

Beat the egg in a shallow bowl suitable for dipping. In another bowl, combine the flour, salt and pepper. In a third flat dish, mix together the Parmesan cheese, oatmeal and basil. Dredge each chicken breast in the flour mixture and shake off excess. Dip into the egg to coat, then into the cheese mixture.

Place the chicken on the prepared baking sheet and drizzle with melted butter. Bake until chicken is cooked through and juices run clear when pierced, 20 to 30 minutes. Serve warm.

Barbecued Thai Chicken

This thick, dark, sweet sauce makes for one of the best barbecued chicken dishes you've ever tasted. Kejap manis is an Indonesian ketchup sold in the Asian section of grocery stores.

Makes 6 servings

6 chicken breasts, bone in
1 bunch fresh cilantro, chopped

Sauce:
1 cup (250 mL) unsweetened coconut milk
6 tbsp (90 mL) kejap manis
6 tbsp (90 mL) fish sauce
4 tsp (20 mL) packed brown sugar
5 cloves garlic, minced
4 tsp (20 mL) grated fresh gingerroot
1/2 tsp (2 mL) turmeric

Sauce: In a food processor, purée the coconut milk, kejap manis, fish sauce, sugar, garlic, gingerroot and turmeric. Pour over the chicken in a large shallow dish and refrigerate overnight.

Preheat the barbecue to medium-low.

Remove the chicken from marinade and shake off excess. Place on the grill and cook, basting frequently with sauce, for 30 to 40 minutes, or until juices run clear when chicken is pierced. Discard remaining sauce. Garnish with cilantro to serve.

Tandoori-Style Grilled Chicken with Cucumber Cilantro Salad

The word "tandoor" actually refers to a cylindrical clay oven used in India to bake bread and roast meats. In North America, we use this term to describe a type of marinade or rub that's applied to chicken or fish. The yogurt and lemon juice tenderize the chicken while the ginger, garlic and spices give it a ton of flavour and kick. The cucumber salad cools it all down. Serve with basmati rice and a cold bottle of Gewürztraminer and you'll have them coming back for more.

Makes 8 servings

2 lb (1 kg) chicken legs, cut into thighs and drumsticks
2 tbsp (30 mL) finely diced red onion
1 tbsp (15 mL) chopped fresh cilantro

Tandoori Marinade:
2 cups (500 mL) yogurt (preferably Liberty brand, if you can find it)
2 tbsp (30 mL) fresh lemon juice
2 tbsp (30 mL) minced fresh gingerroot
2 cloves garlic, minced
1 tsp (5 mL) ground coriander
1 tsp (5 mL) turmeric
1/2 tsp (2 mL) sea salt
1/2 tsp (2 mL) each paprika, ground cumin, freshly ground pepper
    and cayenne pepper

Cucumber Salad:
1/2 English cucumber, diced (1/2 inch/1 cm)
2 tbsp (30 mL) finely diced red onion
1 tbsp (15 mL) chopped fresh cilantro
1 tbsp (15 mL) olive oil
Sea salt and freshly ground pepper

Tandoori Marinade: In a food processor or blender, combine the yogurt, lemon juice, gingerroot, garlic, coriander, turmeric, salt, paprika, cumin, pepper and cayenne; mix well.

Preheat the barbecue to medium-high.

Place the chicken on the grill and cook just long enough to leave grill marks on both sides (do not cook through). Remove from heat and refrigerate until cool. Cover chicken with half of the Tandoori Marinade. Cover and refrigerate overnight. (Because you have only partially cooked the chicken, you must keep it refrigerated until you finish the cooking; do not leave the chicken out once you have put the grill marks on it.) Refrigerate remaining Tandoori Marinade separately.

Preheat the oven to 350°F (180°C).

Remove the chicken from the marinade, shaking off excess. Discard marinade. Place the chicken on a baking sheet and bake, uncovered, for 20 minutes; turn chicken pieces and bake until cooked through and juices run clear when pierced, 15 to 20 minutes longer.

Cucumber Salad: In a bowl, toss together the cucumber, onion, cilantro, oil, and salt and pepper to taste.

Place the chicken in a serving dish and sprinkle with the diced red onion and chopped cilantro. Serve with Cucumber Salad and reserved Tandoori Marinade on the side.

Red Wine–Braised Duck Legs with Orange Zest and Olives

Braising is the preferred method for cooking duck legs; a long, slow simmer is required to tenderize them. The combination of the orange, red wine and olives stands up to the richness of the duck without taking over the dish. I serve this with Chèvre Mashed Potatoes (page 136) and a huge dish of sautéed spinach.

Makes 6 servings

2 tsp (10 mL) sea salt
2 cloves garlic
3 sprigs fresh thyme, leaves only
2 tsp (10 mL) freshly ground pepper
Pinch red pepper flakes
6 duck legs
3 tbsp (45 mL) extra-virgin olive oil
1 large onion, diced
1 carrot, diced
1 leek (white part only), halved lengthwise, then sliced 1/4 inch (5 mm) thick
2 cups (500 mL) dry red wine
1 cup (250 mL) diced seeded peeled tomatoes
1/2 bunch fresh parsley
4 sprigs fresh thyme
1 bay leaf
1 tbsp (15 mL) grated orange zest
4 cups (1 L) chicken stock
Sea salt
1 to 2 tbsp (15 to 30 mL) butter
1 cup (250 mL) green olives, preferably Picholine or Arbequina
Grated orange zest and chopped fresh thyme

Using a mortar and pestle, crush together the salt, garlic, thyme, pepper and red pepper flakes. Rub the underside of each duck leg with the spice mixture. Refrigerate overnight.

In a large heavy pot, heat the oil over high heat; sear the duck legs, skin side down, until nicely browned. Turn over and sear until other side is browned, 10 to 20 minutes total. Transfer the duck to a platter. Remove the skin.

Pour off all but 3 tbsp (45 mL) fat from pot; cook the onion, carrot and leek over medium-high heat, stirring frequently, until browned and tender, 8 to 10 minutes. Add the red wine, tomatoes, parsley, thyme, bay leaf and orange zest; bring to a boil. Reduce heat to simmer and cook until reduced by half.

Return the duck legs to the pot and pour in the stock to cover; bring to a boil. Skim off any visible fat from the surface. Reduce heat, cover and simmer until very tender, 30 to 40 minutes.

Remove the duck legs from the pot. Strain the cooking liquid and return liquid to pot; bring to a boil. Skim off the excess fat and reduce until it coats the back of a spoon. Taste and add salt if necessary. Stir in the butter to taste. Add the olives and duck legs. Garnish with additional orange zest and thyme and serve immediately.

Theme Parties During the 1980s, theme parties were all the rage: Champagne and Chocolate Parties, Pasta Parties, Fondue Parties, Omelette Brunches and even Submarine Sandwich Soirées. These gatherings were tons of fun, but they took a fair amount of orchestrating and often required special equipment. Our favourite theme was desserts, where we really shone. We offered the spectacular, the decadent, the delicious: concord cakes and lemon dacquoise, chocolate berets and budinos, papaya passion fruit tarts and strawberry trees. We even catered a few dessert-only weddings – my kind of party!

Chapter Five

MAINS: SEAFOOD

Perfectly fresh seafood is delicious all on its own, but here are a few ways to make it even better. From martini marinades to sugar-smoking, we have a lot of fun making seafood special.

On the West Coast we're very spoiled, as we have access to such a wide array of fresh seafood year-round: wild spring salmon from Campbell River, Dungeness crab from Clayoquot Sound and halibut from the Queen Charlottes. In summer, our family spends time on one of the islands up the coast, so we have the opportunity to catch crabs and salmon, buy prawns right off the commercial fishing boats and dig clams from the beachfront. It's hard to beat this, I know, but thankfully shipping methods are so efficient you can have fresh lobsters shipped from one side of the country to the other in a day. We're all getting better access to the bounty the two coasts provide. As wild salmon has been a staple on our menu at LSFF and as it's available in most areas of the country, I have included several recipes. Although my preference is always to use fresh rather than frozen, wild salmon is one fish that freezes quite well – the fat content is high, preventing the fish from drying out. It barbecues beautifully but is equally delicious sautéed, poached or baked, sauced or marinated. Many of you will be thrilled to see the recipe for Dungeness Crab Cakes with Lemon Tomato Aïoli, another signature LSFF dish. The Lemon Caper Snapper can easily be made with any white fish, although I'm not keen on frozen white fish as the oil content is often low and the fish can end up with a spongy texture. When it comes to seafood, unless you have no other option, always try to buy fresh.

Oven-Roasted Salmon with Leek and Preserved Lemon Confit

On the West Coast, we're crazy about salmon and can be very particular about where it comes from. At LSFF, we've cooked and served a lot of wild salmon, and although we did try farmed salmon, we quickly returned to the wild variety for several reasons – not the least of which is the far superior taste and texture. And that's not even getting into the politics of farmed salmon, which is a whole other chapter!

Makes 8 servings

3 lb (1.5 kg) wild salmon, divided into 8 portions
   (each about 6 oz/180 g), skin removed
Olive oil
Sea salt and freshly ground pepper
2 tsp (10 mL) lemon balm (or chives), julienned

Preserved Lemon Confit:
1 leek
3 tsp (15 mL) unsalted butter
Sea salt and freshly ground pepper
Rind of 2 preserved lemons (see Seven-Day Preserved Lemons, page 178),
   rinsed and finely minced
2 tsp (10 mL) fresh lemon juice

Preheat the oven to 375°F (190°C).

Brush each piece of salmon with oil and season to taste with salt and pepper. In an ovenproof sauté pan over high heat, sear the salmon for about 15 seconds per side. Transfer to oven and bake until still slightly translucent in the centre but opaque elsewhere, 8 to 10 minutes.

Preserved Lemon Confit: Wash the leek thoroughly. Thinly slice the white part and about 2 inches (5 cm) of the green part. In a skillet, melt 2 tsp (10 mL) of the butter over low heat; sauté the leeks until soft, 5 to 10 minutes. Season to taste with salt and pepper. Add the preserved lemon rind and juice. Stir in the remaining butter.

To serve, spoon a dollop of the Preserved Lemon Confit over each piece of salmon and garnish with lemon balm.

LSFF Dungeness Crab Cakes with Lemon Tomato Aïoli

From the first day we opened our store, these crab cakes were a real hit – so much so that we can never take them off the menu. My husband says it's because they're crab cakes with real crab! So many crab cakes are packed with filler.

Makes 6 crab cakes

1 1/2 lb (750 g) Dungeness crabmeat, well drained, all shell removed
2 green onions
1/3 sweet red pepper, finely diced
1/3 sweet yellow pepper, finely diced
3 eggs, beaten
3/4 cup (175 mL) fresh fine white bread crumbs
2 tbsp (30 mL) olive oil
1 tbsp (15 mL) unsalted butter
Lemon Tomato Aïoli (recipe follows)

Coating:
2 large eggs
1 cup (250 mL) dry white bread crumbs

In a bowl, mix together the crabmeat, green onions and red and yellow peppers. Add the beaten eggs and fresh bread crumbs. Using hands, mix well and form into 6 cakes, each about 1 inch (2.5 cm) thick and 4 inches (10 cm) in diameter. (For perfectly shaped crab cakes, use a round cookie cutter as a guide. Place the cookie cutter on a baking sheet lined with parchment paper or plastic wrap. Press the crabmeat into the cutter, then pull it up. Repeat 5 times.)

Coating: In a shallow dish suitable for dipping, beat the eggs. Place the dry bread crumbs in another shallow dish. Gently dip each crab cake into the egg mixture, then into the bread crumbs, turning to coat. Repeat the process so that each crab cake gets dipped twice. Refrigerate on a baking sheet until ready to cook.

In a large sauté pan, heat the oil and butter over medium-low until just bubbling; cook the crab cakes until golden brown, 3 to 4 minutes per side. Serve warm with Lemon Tomato Aïoli.

Aïoli is a staple in our kitchen. It packs a ton of flavour, so it's great to serve with raw veggies, sneak into a sandwich or slather on a crab cake.

Lemon Tomato Aïoli

Makes 2 1/2 cups (625 mL)

2 cups (500 mL) mayonnaise
Grated zest of 1 lemon
1 tbsp (15 mL) fresh lemon juice
2 roma tomatoes, seeded and finely diced
1/4 cup (50 mL) minced sun-dried tomatoes
3 cloves garlic, minced
Dash Tabasco sauce

In a bowl, stir together the mayonnaise, lemon zest and juice, roma tomatoes, sun-dried tomatoes, garlic and Tabasco sauce. Refrigerate until ready to use.

Grilled Ponzu Salmon with Napa Cabbage and Pea Shoot Slaw

The cabbage and pea shoot slaw is a fresh contrast to the salmon, which is rich, salty and sweet in this marinade. If you can't find pea shoots, substitute julienned snowpeas. Napa cabbage is available at most vegetable markets or grocery stores.

Makes 8 servings

3 lb (1.5 kg) wild salmon, divided into 8 portions (each about 6 oz/180 g)

Ponzu Marinade:
1 1/2 cups (375 mL) freshly squeezed orange juice
1 cup (250 mL) soy sauce
6 oz (180 mL) sake
1/3 cup (75 mL) sugar
3 tbsp (45 mL) fresh lime juice
Pinch red pepper flakes

Napa Cabbage and Pea Shoot Slaw:
1/4 cup (50 mL) thinly sliced red cabbage
1/4 cup (50 mL) thinly sliced napa cabbage
1 carrot, julienned
1 green onion, thinly sliced
1/2 cup (125 mL) pea shoots
2 tbsp (30 mL) fresh lime juice
2 tbsp (30 mL) rice wine vinegar
2 tbsp (30 mL) chopped fresh cilantro
Sea salt and freshly ground pepper

Ponzu Marinade: In a heavy saucepan over medium-high heat, combine the orange juice, soy sauce, sake, sugar, lime juice and chili flakes; bring to a boil. Reduce heat and simmer until reduced by one-third. Let cool before pouring over the salmon in a shallow glass dish. Marinate the salmon in the refrigerator for 1 hour.

Napa Cabbage and Pea Shoot Slaw: In a large bowl, combine the red and napa cabbage, carrot, onion, pea shoots, lime juice, rice wine vinegar and cilantro. Mix well and let marinate for 1 hour. Season to taste with salt and pepper.

Preheat the grill to medium-high.

Remove salmon from marinade and place on the grill; cook until fish flakes easily with fork, about 8 minutes per inch (2.5 cm) of thickness, turning halfway through cooking time. Top each serving of salmon with Napa Cabbage and Pea Shoot Slaw and serve immediately.

Lime Cilantro Grilled Halibut Steaks

Simple, fresh and quick, this is a great way to serve fish in the summer. Try it with tuna steaks as well. If you like, turn up the heat with a few chopped jalapeño peppers mixed into the butter.

Makes 8 servings

8 halibut steaks, about 3 lb (1.5 kg) total (if large, serve half a steak per person)
Juice of 3 limes
1/2 cup (125 mL) extra-virgin olive oil
1/2 cup (125 mL) chopped fresh cilantro
4 tbsp (60 mL) unsalted butter, at room temperature
Lime wedges

Place halibut steaks in a shallow dish and sprinkle with the lime juice, oil and cilantro. Marinate in the refrigerator for 2 hours, turning the fish occasionally.

Prepare hot coals with a generous amount of mesquite for grilling. Remove the fish from the marinade, reserving marinade, and place on the grill. Cook, turning the fish once and basting occasionally with the reserved marinade, until it flakes easily with a fork, about 5 minutes per side. Transfer to a warmed serving platter. Spread the butter over the fish. Garnish with lime wedges.

Sugar-Smoked Tuna with Papaya Lime Salsa

Tuna is a very meaty fish that stands up well to different treatments. The smoking adds another dimension to the flavour, but make sure you don't overcook it; tuna should always be served on the rare side or else it will be very dry. Salmon is also fabulous done this way. This can be cooked on the stovetop too, but make sure the fan is on high.

Makes 6 servings

1/2 cup (125 mL) packed brown sugar
1/4 cup (50 mL) brewed black tea
Grated zest of 1 lemon
1 tbsp (15 mL) fennel seed
1 tbsp (15 mL) dried thyme
1 tbsp (15 mL) coriander seeds
6 tuna steaks, each 5 oz (150 g)
Olive oil
Sea salt and freshly ground pepper
Papaya Lime Salsa (recipe follows)

Preheat the barbecue to high.

Line a heavy-bottomed roasting pan with foil. Spread the sugar, tea, lemon zest, fennel seed, thyme and coriander seeds over the foil. Place a cooling rack in the pan over the spices. Brush the tuna steaks with oil and sprinkle with salt and pepper; place on the rack. Tightly cover the pan with foil. Place on the grill and cook until the sugar melts and starts to smoke, about 2 minutes. Reduce heat to low and cook until medium-rare, 3 to 5 minutes. Serve with a generous dollop of Papaya Lime Salsa.

Papaya Lime Salsa

Makes 2 cups (250 mL)

This salsa works equally well on salmon or halibut. It would also be fabulous on grilled chicken when you're looking for a light summer entrée that's full of flavour and colour.

1 papaya, peeled, seeded and diced (1/2-inch/1 cm cubes)
2 limes, peeled, seeded and diced (1/2-inch/1 cm pieces)
1 orange, peeled, sectioned and cut into 1/2-inch (1 cm) pieces
1/2 red onion, finely diced
Juice of 4 limes
1/4 cup (50 mL) olive oil
6 large fresh basil leaves
Sea salt and freshly ground pepper

In a bowl, combine the papaya, limes, orange and onion. Pour in the lime juice and oil. Toss gently. Just before serving, julienne the basil and stir in. Season to taste with salt and pepper.

Lemon Caper Snapper

We should all eat more fish, and this recipe makes it more fun: sweet, salty, nutty...yum. Don't stop at snapper; try using halibut, cod, sole or trout. If the fish fillets are thin, reduce the marinating time. Serve with basmati or wild rice and A Basket of Cherry Tomatoes with Basil and Cream (page 126).

Makes 6 servings

2 1/4 lb (1.125 kg) red snapper, orange roughy or cod fillets, divided into 6 portions
   (each about 6 oz/180 g)
Salt and freshly ground pepper
1/3 cup (75 mL) golden raisins
1/3 cup (75 mL) capers, drained
2 tbsp (30 mL) pine nuts, toasted
Grated zest of 2 lemons

Marinade:
2/3 cup (150 mL) olive oil
1/3 cup (75 mL) fresh lemon juice
1 tbsp (15 mL) balsamic vinegar

Marinade: In a bowl, whisk together the oil, lemon juice and vinegar; set aside.

Season the fish fillets with salt and pepper. Place in a shallow dish and pour half of the marinade over top. Cover and marinate in refrigerator for 1 hour. Refrigerate reserved marinade separately.

Preheat the oven to 200°F (100°C) and place a platter inside to warm.

Heat a nonstick skillet over high heat. Remove the fillets from the marinade and place them in the skillet, making sure they don't touch. (You may need to use 2 skillets.) Reduce heat to medium-high; cook the fish for 1 to 2 minutes, depending on the thickness, then turn and cook until just barely done, about 5 minutes.

Transfer the fish to the warm platter and cover with foil; set aside. Pour the reserved marinade into the same skillet and add the raisins and capers; heat through. Pour over the fish and garnish with pine nuts and lemon zest.

Martini-Marinated Seafood Skewers with Cilantro Sauce

This is a spectacular party dish, not just because it's marinated in the ingredients that go into your favourite cocktail, but because it can be made ahead and is easy to multiply. In the summer, throw these skewers on the barbecue; in the winter, just stick them under the broiler. To serve them as an hors d'oeuvre, cut back to one scallop and one prawn per skewer. Thread the prawn first, so it curls around the scallop. Serve the Cilantro Sauce as a dip on the side. Then all you'll need is a martini in hand, and since you already have the vodka and vermouth out, why not?

Makes 9 servings

27 prawns, peeled and deveined
18 scallops

Marinade:
2 tsp (10 mL) grated lemon zest
2 cups (500 mL) fresh lemon juice
2 tbsp (30 mL) vermouth
2 tbsp (30 mL) vodka
2 tbsp (30 mL) olive oil

Cilantro Sauce:
2 cups (500 mL) loosely packed fresh cilantro
1 cup (250 mL) vegetable oi
1/2 cup (125 mL) orange juice concentrate
1 tbsp (15 mL) fresh lemon juice
4 tsp (20 mL) ground cumin
1 tbsp (15 mL) mayonnaise
Sea salt and freshly ground pepper
Cayenne pepper

Alternately thread prawns and scallops (3 prawns and 2 scallops per skewer) onto each of 9 skewers. Place skewers in a shallow baking dish.

Marinade: In a bowl, mix together the lemon zest and juice, vermouth, vodka and oil. Pour marinade over skewers in pan; cover and marinate in the refrigerator for 30 minutes or for up to 1 hour (no longer or else the seafood will begin to "cook" in the lemon juice).

Cilantro Sauce: Meanwhile, in a food processor, combine the cilantro, oil, orange juice concentrate, lemon juice and cumin. Stir in the mayonnaise. Season to taste with salt, pepper and cayenne. Cover and refrigerate until ready to use.

Preheat the barbecue to medium-high.

Remove the skewers from the marinade and place on the grill. Cook until the scallops and prawns are opaque, about 2 minutes per side. Serve with Cilantro Sauce on the side.

Three Weddings

Everyone knows that on the wet West Coast you should not plan an outdoor wedding without a backup plan. Especially when the wedding reception is a sit-down garden lunch for more than 100 people and an enormous cherry tree in the centre of the yard prevents the tent from covering all the tables.

September is usually the most reliable month for decent weather, but, of course, on that particular day we awoke to grey skies, which everyone tried to ignore until the rain did start to fall and enormous green garbage bags had to be stretched over everything. Thankfully, it rained for only a couple of hours. By the time the reception started, the skies had cleared, and we were spared the umbrella brigade and ruined shoes. The day was so humid, though, that the wedding cake, a tower of choux pastry and caramel known as a croquembouche, was a casualty. Arriving well after the appointed hour, the croquembouche proceeded to cave in on itself; fortunately the maid of honour had the presence of mind to put her bouquet on top, so no one was the wiser.

This was not the first hiccup in the wedding plans; the day before, we received the news that there was no fresh Dungeness crabmeat to be found in the city. This was a bit depressing, considering we'd spent two months collecting and washing enough crab shells to serve Chilled Dungeness Crab. And, of course, the menus had already been printed. We had no choice but to trust the seafood suppliers, who assured us that fresh-frozen crab would be delicious. We carried on, changing the focus to the organic wild greens, flowers and baby vegetables served with the crab. The bride knew everyone would be impressed by the individual crème brûlée tarts garnished with hand-picked blackberries; unfortunately, she was so busy talking during dessert that her plate was whisked away before she could indulge.

The moral of the story?
Never cater your best friend's wedding.

The second most memorable wedding I've catered took place in the month of June, when you're almost guaranteed to see some rain on the West Coast. Nevertheless, the bride insisted on the date and chose a fabulous farm in the city as the venue. We spent two glorious hot, sunny days decorating the barn and marquee with flowers and foliage from the gardens of everyone we knew. The big day arrived in all its sobering grey; the rain held off just long enough to allow the bride to walk down the aisle. At the reception, everyone dined well on antipasto platters, rack of lamb and fondant-draped chocolate wedding cake. The rain continued to fall late into the night; guests dodged the rain buckets on the barn dance floor. It was a cozy evening! We had to rely on flashlights and candlelight to set the mood, as lighting had yet to be installed in the barn. But still, 10 years later, we remember that wedding fondly.

The moral of the story?
Be wary of catering your own sister's wedding.

Wedding number three of note was my brother's, which was profoundly affected by weather but in a very different way. CedarCreek, a well-known Okanagan winery owned by close friends, seemed like the perfect spot for an intimate family wedding, especially because the groom was in the wine business and the bride's mother lived nearby. There was a lot of planning: I had to orchestrate getting all the food and service staff from Vancouver to Kelowna on time, then transform the outdoor marquee into an alfresco dining experience.

Unfortunately, this was the summer of 2003: there was not a drop of rain, and forest fires ravaged the Okanagan. Luck and resources saved Cedar-Creek Estate Winery from burning to the ground, but as a result of the fires, the wedding had to be relocated to Vancouver and held outdoors in a friend's garden. Because we didn't have to transport everything quite so far, we enjoyed a slightly more ambitious menu. Luckily, my mother doesn't have to worry about any more family weddings and, better still, neither do I.

The moral of the story?
If you hadn't learned from catering your best friend's and your sister's weddings, either you have a masochistic streak or just can't say no. Always have an alternative plan in your back pocket.

Chapter Six
VEGETABLES

Crisp and fresh or rich and luscious, vegetables go far beyond the standard side dish. It may be a simple twist on a classic dish, or a delicious sauce on a new favourite – here the veggies really shine.

Most people get stuck when trying to create new ways to prepare and serve vegetables. Potatoes are among the easiest ones to work with; they're readily available and they work well with so many flavours and textures. Now there are more and more kinds available as farmers bring back heirloom varieties. The Yukon Gold has become the new darling of the mashed potato world because of the creamy texture and rich yellow flesh. Others to look for and experiment with are the Red Bliss, Nova Scotia Blue and Straight Banana.

I like to explore new cooking methods for other vegetables, too. Try roasting green beans until they're almost crispy. Cherry tomatoes are traditionally eaten in a salad or on a veggie platter, but in A Basket of Cherry Tomatoes with Basil and Cream, they're baked to concentrate the tomato flavour, then transformed into a luxurious dish with a finish of heavy cream. Serve them with steak right off the grill and you have a perfect summer dinner. Another vegetable I've highlighted is the eggplant; it's often neglected and misunderstood in North America, yet it's loved and appreciated all over Europe. Try the Japanese eggplant first; it's usually less bitter and contains less water.

In the summer months, when the oven is off and the barbecue is on, grill your veggies. Potatoes and root veggies, such as carrots, will fare better if they're parboiled first, but most green vegetables can simply be brushed with olive oil, sprinkled with salt and pepper and thrown on the barbecue.

Grilled Tuscan Vegetables with Balsamic Vinaigrette

Along with our Dungeness Crab Cakes, this dish was on our menu the first day our store opened, and it's been a staple ever since. Not only is it easy to prep ahead but it's also versatile – it goes well with lots of main courses. Use your imagination and try other vegetables, like asparagus or mushrooms. Leftover veggies are delicious in salads and sandwiches.

There will be extra vinaigrette, so you can add more veggies if you're feeding a crowd, or use what's left over on leafy green salads. Another option: for an amazing first course, toss the vinaigrette with grilled mushrooms, baby spinach, candied salmon and chèvre. The vinaigrette will keep for several weeks in the refrigerator.

Makes 8 servings

3 zucchinis, sliced 1/4 inch (5 mm) thick
2 eggplants, sliced 1/4 inch (5 mm) thick
3 sweet yellow peppers, cut in half and cored
3 sweet red peppers, cut in half and cored
1 small red onion, cut into rings
Sea salt and freshly ground pepper

Balsamic Vinaigrette:
1/4 cup (50 mL) balsamic vinegar
2 tsp (10 mL) grainy mustard
1 clove garlic, minced
1/2 tsp (2 mL) finely chopped fresh rosemary
1/4 tsp (1 mL) fresh thyme leaves
3/4 cup (175 mL) extra-virgin olive oil
Sea salt and freshly ground pepper

Preheat grill or barbecue to medium-high.

Balsamic Vinaigrette: Whisk together the vinegar, mustard, garlic, rosemary and thyme. Gradually add the oil, whisking constantly, until mixture thickens slightly. Season to taste with salt and pepper.

Place the zucchini, eggplant, yellow and red peppers and onion on the grill; cook, turning occasionally, until cooked through and nicely charred. The peppers and onions will take twice as long as the zucchini and eggplant. Remove from the grill. Cut the peppers in half crosswise, and then into strips.

Place the grilled vegetables in a bowl and toss with enough vinaigrette to coat. Season to taste with salt and pepper. Serve at room temperature.

A Basket of Cherry Tomatoes with Basil and Cream

Summertime in British Columbia is amazing for all the local produce that's available. It's hard to resist feeding family and friends as much of it as possible since the season is so fleeting. This is an ultra-easy dish for when you want to add a little extra to those sweet 100s, or grape and cherry tomatoes we're seeing a lot of these days. They're perfect with any kind of roasted or grilled meat, fish or leftovers, and they warm up nicely the next day for adding to rice or pasta. The recipe multiplies well, as long as you don't put the tomatoes in more than one layer in the pan; they can touch, just not be piled on top of each other.

Makes 6 to 8 servings

1 1/2 pint baskets cherry tomatoes (about 3 cups/750 mL)
2 tbsp (30 mL) olive oil
Sea salt and freshly ground pepper
1/4 cup (50 mL) heavy cream
3 tbsp (45 mL) shredded fresh basil

Preheat the oven to 350°F (180°C).

In a small roasting pan or baking pan, drizzle the tomatoes with oil. Sprinkle with salt and pepper to taste. Roast for 20 minutes. Pour in the cream and sprinkle with the basil; cook, stirring gently occasionally, until thickened slightly and cream is evaporated, 10 to 15 minutes. Serve warm.

Oven-Roasted Green Beans with Pancetta

This is one of the simplest, most delicious ways to serve green beans in the summer, when you can pick or buy the brilliant skinny ones.

Makes 6 servings

1 lb (500 g) green beans, trimmed
1 tbsp (15 mL) olive oil
Sea salt and freshly ground pepper
2 oz (60 g) pancetta
1/4 small red onion

Preheat the oven to 375°F (190°C).

Spread the beans on a baking sheet and drizzle with the oil. Sprinkle with salt and pepper and roast for 10 minutes.

Meanwhile, dice the pancetta and slice the onion into thin strips. Remove the pan from the oven; sprinkle the pancetta and red onion over the beans; toss to combine and return to oven. Roast until the beans are just slightly brown, the onions wilted and the pancetta a bit brown, 5 to 10 minutes. Serve immediately.

Spicy Chiang Mai Green Beans

This dish is particularly good in the summer, when green beans are at their peak – that means thin, tender and almost always local. Kick them up a notch (as Emeril would say) with this chili garlic cashew version.

Makes 6 servings

2 tbsp (30 mL) cashews
3 tbsp (45 mL) vegetable oil
2 cloves garlic, minced
2 tbsp (30 mL) sambal oelek*
2 tbsp (30 mL) fish sauce*
1 tbsp (15 mL) packed brown sugar
1 lb (500 g) green beans, stem ends removed

Preheat the oven to 325°F (160°C). Spread the cashews on a baking sheet and toast until light golden, 5 to 10 minutes. Let cool. Chop coarsely.

In a heavy skillet, heat oil over medium heat; gently cook the garlic until light golden. Add the sambal oelek, fish sauce and sugar and cook, stirring, for 1 minute. Increase heat to high; add the green beans and sauté until tender-crisp, 1 to 2 minutes. Remove from heat. Toss in the cashews and serve.

* Sambal oelek and fish sauce can be found
in the Asian foods section of many large grocery stores.

Broccolini with Mustard Caper Butter

Broccolini is a new vegetable, a hybrid made from crossing Chinese kale and broccoli. (You may also see it under the name Aspiration.) It's a little sweet and a little bitter. The stems are long and slim, and the flower heads are smaller than broccoli heads. The mustard caper butter is a fast way to add interest to broccolini or regular broccoli.

Makes 6 servings

1 lb (500 g) broccolini or broccoli
4 tbsp (60 mL) unsalted butter, softened
1 tbsp (15 mL) grainy mustard
1 tbsp (15 mL) capers, drained
Sea salt and freshly ground pepper

Trim the ends of the broccolini. Pour enough water into a saucepan to come 2 inches (5 cm) up side of pan. Place broccolini in a steamer basket and set in saucepan. Cover, bring to a boil and simmer until broccolini loses its crunch but is still slightly firm, 2 to 3 minutes.

Meanwhile, in a bowl, mix together the butter, mustard, capers, and salt and pepper to taste. Remove the broccolini from heat, drain well and serve immediately with a dollop of the Mustard Caper Butter on each serving.

Roasted Cauliflower When the barbecue goes away for the winter and we turn the oven back on, I favour roasting vegetables over boiling or steaming them. Roasting cauliflower gives it a nice nutty flavour. Preheat the oven to 375°F (190°C), cut the cauliflower into small florets and toss with olive oil, sea salt and a touch of sugar, cayenne and nutmeg. Roast for 15 to 20 minutes, stirring once or twice to ensure even cooking. Serve warm.

Roasted Eggplant Bread Pudding with Charred Tomato Vinaigrette

Don't be afraid of this recipe because it seems like too much work. And don't dismiss it for being too bizarre. Putting eggplant and pudding in the same sentence is a bit of a surprise, but believe me, it's great. At LSFF, we often make savoury bread puddings as an alternative to other starches. This one is excellent as a side dish at dinner or at brunch, to serve with Boursin and leek omelettes and the Pastel Fruit Salad on page 41.

Makes 6 servings

1/2 loaf day-old sourdough bread
1 eggplant (about 1/2 lb/250 g), peeled and cut into 1-inch (2.5 cm) cubes
2 tbsp (30 mL) olive oil
3 large cloves garlic, minced
1 large leek, chopped
3/4 cup (175 mL) chopped peeled tomatoes
1 cup (250 mL) grated Parmesan cheese
3 tbsp (45 mL) chopped fresh basil
5 large eggs
1 1/4 cups (300 mL) milk
Sea salt and freshly ground pepper

Preheat the oven to 375°F (190°C).

Oil an 8-inch (20 cm) square pan or 2-quart (2 L) soufflé dish; you'll need either a dish with a lid or sufficient foil to cover.

Cut bread into 1-inch (2.5 cm) cubes and spread on a baking sheet. Toast in the oven until light golden brown, about 5 minutes. Set aside. Toss the eggplant with 1 tbsp (15 mL) of the oil. Roast until tender, 15 to 20 minutes. Set aside, leaving oven on.

In a large skillet, heat the remaining tbsp (15 mL) oil over medium heat; sauté the garlic and leek until soft and golden.

In a large bowl, combine the bread cubes, eggplant, leek mixture, tomatoes, 1/2 cup (125 mL) of the Parmesan cheese and basil; mix well. In a separate large bowl, whisk the eggs with milk; season to taste with salt and pepper. Combine the eggplant and egg mixtures, tossing well to combine. Pour into the prepared pan. Sprinkle with the remaining Parmesan cheese. Cover and bake for 40 minutes. Uncover and bake until golden and set, about 10 minutes. Serve with Charred Tomato Vinaigrette.

Charred Tomato Vinaigrette

1/2 lb (250 g) Italian plum tomatoes
3/4 cup (175 mL) olive oil
1/4 cup (50 mL) balsamic vinegar
1/4 tsp (1 mL) sea salt
1/8 tsp (0.5 mL) freshly ground pepper

Preheat the barbecue to high heat or preheat the broiler. Grill or broil the tomatoes, turning occasionally, until charred on all sides. In a food processor, purée the tomatoes with skins on. With machine running, add the oil and vinegar, mixing well. Mix in the salt and pepper. Refrigerate until ready to use.

Japanese Eggplant with Garlic and Chèvre

You can roast the eggplants under the broiler or barbecue them for extra flavour. Roasted garlic oil adds depth of flavour to this dish as well as to grilled meats and salad dressings. The remaining garlic oil can be refrigerated for up to one week to use in salad dressings or to brush on grilled meats. If you don't have time to roast the garlic, as a shortcut add 1 clove garlic, crushed, to the 2 tbsp (30 mL) olive oil you brush on the eggplant.

Makes 6 servings

12 cloves garlic (unpeeled), halved lengthwise
2 sprigs fresh thyme
Extra-virgin olive oil
3 large Japanese eggplants
1/4 tsp (1 mL) sea salt
1/2 tsp (2 mL) sugar
6 oz (180 g) chèvre, crumbled
6 sun-dried tomatoes, julienned

In a small deep pot, combine the garlic and thyme; pour in enough of the oil to cover. Bring to a low simmer and cook until exposed cloves turn a very pale golden brown and are soft enough to push out of the peel with little effort, about 30 minutes. Drain the hot oil into a heatproof container.

Peel and coarsely chop the garlic; toss with 2 tbsp (30 mL) roasted garlic oil, sea salt and sugar. Set aside. Refrigerate the remaining garlic oil for up to 1 week.

Preheat the barbecue to medium or preheat the broiler, placing the rack 6 inches (15 cm) below the heat.

Cut each eggplant in half lengthwise. Score a crisscross pattern in the cut side of each. Brush the cut sides with a little of the roasted garlic oil mixture. Place cut side down on the grill and cook until soft, about 5 minutes. Turn over and cook for 2 minutes longer. If broiling, cook for the same amount of time but start with eggplants cut side up. Remove from heat.

Arrange each eggplant half on a serving dish, cut side up. Sprinkle with the reserved chopped garlic, chèvre and sun-dried tomatoes to serve.

Roasted Breast of Chicken with Garlic and Candied Lemon (page 100)

Grilled Ponzu Salmon with Napa Cabbage and Pea Shoot Slaw (page 114)

Grilled Tuscan Vegetables with Balsamic Vinaigrette (page 125)

Breakfast Cookies (page 145)

Apple Caramel Crostata with Red Wine Caramel (page 154)

Figs Poached in Chianti with Zabaglione (page 163)

Crispy Sugared Won Ton Leaves with Pumpkin Cream and Maple Syrup (page 166)

Death By Chocolate with Raspberry Splash (page 168)

Tuscan Potato Cakes

We're always searching for and trying new ways to prepare the noble
spud. This dish is a great marriage
of potato, pancetta (or bacon) and
onion. Starting in cold water ensures
even cooking as the potatoes and
water heat up together.

Makes eight 3-inch (8.5 cm) cakes

1 lb (500 g) russet or Idaho baking potatoes
2 tbsp (30 mL) finely diced red onion
1 oz (30 g) pancetta, finely diced
Sea salt and freshly ground pepper
Olive oil

In a saucepan, cover the potatoes with cold water and bring to a boil.
Cook until just tender on the edges and firm in the centre (parboiled),
about 10 minutes. Drain and let cool. Peel the potatoes (it may be easier
to use a knife than a vegetable peeler); grate coarsely into a bowl.

Beginning with a cold skillet, warm the onion and pancetta over medium
heat until onion is soft and fat has melted out of the pancetta. Add to
the grated potato and season to taste with salt and pepper. Scoop the
potato mixture into 3-inch (8.5 cm) round discs onto a baking sheet or
plate. The cakes can be refrigerated, uncooked, for up to 8 hours.

Pour enough of the oil into a sauté pan to just cover the bottom of the
pan; sauté the potato cakes over medium-high heat until golden brown,
about 5 minutes per side. Serve hot.

Party Tips

Entertaining at home is such a great way to connect with family and friends and slow down our frenzied world. For a meal that's memorable, take the time to add some special touches, not only to your cooking but also to your table. Place cards, napkin rings and knife rests are extras that are often forgotten or just skipped. I love arranging place cards on the table; it's a chance to stop and think about where to seat guests in order to stimulate the best conversation. Also, place cards prevent that awkward moment when everyone arrives at the table and wonders where to sit. There are so many creative options besides traditional cards. One of my favourites is to cut a sliver in a pear and insert the card into it, then use a copper plant label for writing the guest's name where the plant name would be. Get your children to help attach gift tags or wine labels to napkins using ribbon or raffia strands. At Easter and Christmas, the children help me make large sugar cookies, and we decorate them with the names of our guests.

If you don't own knife rests, get creative and use flat rocks, chopstick rests or shells. Ribbon, cording and raffia work well for making napkin rings; add flowers, leaves, grasses, herbs or shells. Finally, if you really want to impress everyone, print up the menu and make a couple of copies for the table.

Friends and clients often ask me how they can give their party a more polished look.

I always go back to my mantra: keep it simple. Whether we're talking about the food, presentation or decor, more is not better. You don't need to have six salads for a buffet dinner. Instead, have two or three really amazing ones and make each totally different. For example, you could make the Grilled Potato Salad with Crispy Pancetta, Green Beans and Lemon Dijon Vinaigrette (page 44), then pair it with an oversize platter of vine-ripened tomatoes drizzled with pesto, grilled flank steak and some fabulous bread. Present the flank steak on a huge wooden board and arrange a bunch of watercress, cilantro or Italian parsley in the corner of the board for a simple but dramatic presentation. Make sure the platters and serving bowls will hold slightly more than you have; salads present best when the contents aren't spilling over.

If you're having a multi-course dinner party, keep the hors d'oeuvres to a minimum. My preference is to offer two different types of olives, perhaps niçoise and Picholine, and some warm toasted almonds. Toss whole blanched almonds in enough extra-virgin olive oil to coat, then sprinkle them with coarse sea salt. Roast the almonds in a 350°F (180°C) oven for 5 to 8 minutes and serve warm. (You can also make them ahead and reheat them for a couple of minutes just before serving.)

Serve the olives and almonds in interesting bowls – they don't have to match, but try for a theme that ties them together. For example, use white dishes of different sizes and shapes, or perhaps earthenware dishes of similar colours.

From large pillars in hurricane lamps to tea lights on tiny clay saucers lining a mantel, candles are an inexpensive way to create atmosphere. Be consistent with the look; stick to one colour and arrange them in groupings of odd numbers. Try five pillar candles in different sizes on a coffee table, or tea candles in a row along a windowsill.

I take inspiration from the seasons when I'm setting a table, incorporating items that are easily available. Fall is my favourite season for this; I gather leaves, acorns, chestnuts, rosehips, then buy pears and/or apples. Rather than a formal centrepiece on the table, I create a setting tablescape, with leaves spilling across the table, interspersed with the fruit, chestnuts and other accents. It's fun to do and not difficult, so go ahead and experiment a little. But remember to give yourself enough time – don't start 20 minutes before guests arrive.

When I do want to have flowers on the table, I rarely stick to a single arrangement. I have a collection of vintage canning jars that I fill with tiny clay pots or shells or lemon slices, then pour in water and arrange a small bouquet in each, sticking to one variety of flower in just one or two colours. The effect is much more dramatic; try three shades of pink tulips or white-only daisies or three kinds of sunflowers. Or pull out those martini glasses you've been storing and use them for a table arrangement. Line them along the centre of the table, then float a candle or fully opened rose in each.

On your next trip to the nursery, pick up various sizes of clay pots. Lined with cloth napkins, they're a great alternative to baskets for serving bread, grissini or tortilla chips. I'm always on the hunt for interesting containers for party food. It's even worth checking out spring garage sales for baskets, platters, vases and linens.

Finally, never forget your bathrooms when entertaining. Flowers, candles and pretty guest towels make a real difference. At large parties, a visit to the bathroom is one of the only moments people spend alone, so they do notice the small details. Another nice touch is to put a branch of fresh rosemary or spray of lavender in the wastebasket, especially if it's a wire one.

Chèvre Mashed Potatoes

Yukon Gold potatoes yield a fabulous buttery texture and golden colour. Add chèvre and heavy cream and you'll go absolutely over the top with this recipe. For a lighter version with a bit of a tang, replace the heavy cream with buttermilk. I like to keep the rest of the entrée simple; try grilled steak or chicken along with steamed or grilled vegetables drizzled with balsamic vinegar.

Makes 6 to 8 servings

3 lb (1.5 kg) Yukon Gold potatoes, peeled and cut
    into 2-inch (5 cm) chunks
4 tbsp (60 mL) extra-virgin olive oil
8 oz (250 g) soft chèvre, at room temperature
1/3 cup (75 mL) heavy cream
Sea salt and freshly ground pepper

In a large pot, cover the potatoes with cold water and bring to a boil over medium-high heat. Cook, uncovered, until tender, 20 to 25 minutes.

Drain very well. Purée the potatoes while still piping hot by passing them through a ricer. Mix in the oil and chèvre. Beat in the cream. Season to taste with salt and pepper and serve immediately.

Mashed Potatoes

A potato ricer is a relatively inexpensive investment that pays for itself in accolades the first time you use it. It produces fluffy mashed potatoes without lumps, a better bet than a regular potato masher. After draining the potatoes, return them to the stove just to dry them out a bit more before ricing.

For a change, try using olive oil instead of butter, and buttermilk or yogurt instead of cream. A sprinkle of freshly chopped herbs or a spoonful of pesto or tapenade will turn everyday mashed spuds into a chic starch. If potatoes cool down, they become stodgy, so make sure your ingredients are at room temperature before adding; don't use milk or cream right out of the fridge.

Yukon Gold Potato Galette with Smoked Applewood Cheddar

The smoked Applewood cheddar adds a rich, earthy dimension to this dish. If you can't find it, use a combination of aged cheddar and smoked mozzarella. The smoky flavour of this galette is the perfect complement to roasts of pork, beef or lamb. Like most potato dishes, it's best the day it's made, but can be made earlier in the day and reheated.

Makes 6 servings

3 large Yukon Gold potatoes
1/4 cup (50 mL) butter, melted
1/2 lb (250 g) smoked Applewood cheddar cheese, shredded
1 tsp (5 mL) sea salt
1/4 tsp (1 mL) freshly ground pepper

Preheat the oven to 350°F (180°C). Butter a 9-inch (23 cm) springform pan.

Peel the potatoes and cut into 1/4-inch (5 mm) thick slices. Arrange a layer in the bottom of the pan, overlapping slices slightly. Brush with some of the butter; sprinkle with some of the cheese, salt and pepper. Continue layering in similar manner, ending with a layer of cheese. Bake, covered with foil, for 40 minutes. Remove foil and bake until cheese is golden brown, about 10 minutes.

Rosemary Potato and Prosciutto Gratin

You can never have too many potato recipes – it's akin to women never having too many shoes. Each occasion or entrée demands something different. This dish is a hit with children, even though it's quite rich. I serve it with roast prime rib or beef tenderloin and sautéed spinach for an update on the classic meat and potatoes combo.

Makes 6 servings

4 tbsp (60 mL) olive oil
4 oz (125 g) prosciutto, thinly sliced and cut into strips
2 sprigs fresh rosemary (each about 2 inches/5 cm long)
4 cloves garlic, thinly sliced
2 lb (1 kg) red-skinned potatoes
Sea salt and freshly ground pepper
1 cup (250 mL) heavy cream
1/2 cup (125 mL) grated Parmesan cheese

Preheat the oven to 375°F (190°C).

In a skillet, heat the oil over medium heat; fry the prosciutto until just beginning to crisp. Remove from pan and set aside. Reduce heat to low. Remove the rosemary needles from their stems and stir into the pan along with the garlic; cook for 1 minute. Remove from heat.

Slice the potatoes 1/4 inch (5 mm) thick; place in a large bowl and stir in prosciutto and rosemary mixture. Season to taste with salt and pepper; toss to mix.

Transfer the potato mixture to a baking dish, distributing evenly. Pour cream over top. Cover with foil and bake for 20 minutes. Remove foil and sprinkle with the Parmesan cheese; bake until cream is set and top is brown, about 20 minutes.

Barbecue-Spice Roasted Potatoes

My family likes to barbecue during the summer months, but sometimes we just want the flavour of the 'cue. We serve these potatoes at the pool, at the beach, at bocce and volleyball games and at croquet parties all summer long. Everyone tries to sneak into the kitchen to steal some potatoes just as they come out of the oven.

Makes 6 servings

2 canned chipotle peppers, packed in adobo sauce
4 tbsp (60 mL) olive oil
1 tbsp (15 mL) minced garlic
4 lb (2 kg) small red-skinned potatoes, sliced 1/2 inch (1 cm) thick
1 red onion, separated into rings
2 tbsp (30 mL) chopped fresh cilantro

Spice Mixture:
2 tbsp (30 mL) smoked paprika
1 1/2 tsp (7 mL) chili powder
1 1/2 tsp (7 mL) fennel seeds
3/4 tsp (4 mL) dried sage
3/4 tsp (4 mL) dried basil
1/2 tsp (2 mL) sea salt
1/4 tsp (1 mL) freshly ground pepper

Spice Mixture: In a bowl, combine the paprika, chili powder, fennel seeds, sage, basil, salt and pepper.

Preheat the oven to 350°F (180°C).

Drain the chipotle peppers and purée in a blender; transfer to a large bowl and mix in the Spice Mixture, oil and garlic. Add the potatoes and toss to coat. Spread in a single layer on a baking sheet and roast until tender and slightly crisp.

Grease the grill or barbecue and preheat to medium-high. Place the onion rings on the grill and cook until soft and charred. Transfer to a bowl and add cooked potatoes and cilantro; toss to combine. Serve warm. The potatoes can be made ahead and refrigerated for up to 8 hours. Let come to room temperature before serving.

Chapter Seven

DESSERTS

From cookies and brownies to tarts and custards, desserts have always been our love, and forte, at LSFF. It was very difficult to choose which recipes to include here. These are some of our all-time favourites.

Finally, we come to my favourite chapter. When dining at a restaurant, I'm always the one who wants to look at the dessert menu first – I have an insatiable sweet tooth. I have to know what I'm going to finish with before I pick my main course. This must be why I realized that the selection of desserts available in Vancouver restaurants in the late '80s needed help. So, side by side with the catering business, LSFF started a wholesale dessert division, supplying the chic restaurants in Vancouver with high-end sweets. Once we moved our operation to a storefront location, we were able to offer our desserts to the retail market, too – everything from muffins and scones to mini lemon tarts and decadent chocolate cakes to fruit crostades and meringue confections. For this collection, I've picked a few of our favourites. I hope your taste buds are as satisfied as mine are when you try the Benjamin Bars (named after our pastry chef's first child), the sinfully rich Death by Chocolate or the comforting Caramelized Apple and Rosemary Bread Pudding. As with everything we make, the quality of ingredients is crucial to success, so don't scrimp or substitute when it comes to the basic ingredients: good butter, free-range eggs, unbleached flour and top-quality chocolate. I have always believed that if you're going to the trouble of making something, you must use the best ingredients possible. Then it will be worth every calorie.

Breakfast Cookies

Move over, carb bars! With lots of dried fruits and oats, these breakfast cookies actually taste good and fill the gap. They also freeze beautifully. Go ahead and change the dried fruits and nuts as you like. If you enjoy making cookies, it's worth investing in a small ice cream scoop – it makes scooping the dough faster and easier, with professional results.

Makes 2 dozen large cookies

1 cup (250 mL) unsalted butter
3/4 cup (175 mL) sugar
3/4 cup (175 mL) packed golden brown sugar
2 large eggs
2 cups (500 mL) all-purpose flour
2 cups (500 mL) old fashioned rolled oats
1 tsp (5 mL) sea salt
1/4 tsp (1 mL) baking soda
1 cup (250 mL) chopped toasted pecans
3/4 cup (175 mL) dried tart cherries
1/2 cup (125 mL) chopped dried apricots
1/2 cup (125 mL) chopped dried apples
1/2 cup (125 mL) chopped prunes

Preheat the oven to 350°F (180°C). Line a cookie sheet with parchment paper.

In a large bowl, beat together the butter and white and brown sugars until light and fluffy. Beat in the eggs until well mixed. In a separate bowl, combine the flour, oats, salt and baking soda. In another bowl, combine the pecans, cherries, apricots, apples and prunes. With a large spoon, mix one-quarter of the flour mixture into the butter mixture until combined. Stir in one-quarter of the dried fruit mixture. Add remaining flour and fruit mixtures in 3 more additions, stirring to combine.

Drop the dough by tablespoonfuls (15 mL) onto the prepared cookie sheet. Bake until set and lightly browned, 10 to 15 minutes.

Chewy Brazil Nut and Date Cookies

These cookies are the ultimate hermits. Chock full of nuts and fruit, they're chewy and fragrant, the ideal holiday season treat. I like to make them small and serve them in the afternoon with a strong cup of Darjeeling tea or, for the children, hot chocolate.

Makes 3 dozen medium cookies

1/4 lb (125 g) Brazil nuts, chopped
1/4 lb (125 g) slivered almonds
1 lb (500 g) pitted dates, roughly chopped
1/4 lb (125 g) dried cherries, roughly chopped
1/4 lb (125 g) candied pineapple
1 1/3 cups (325 mL) all-purpose flour
3/4 tsp (4 mL) baking soda
3/4 tsp (4 mL) sea salt
3/4 tsp (4 mL) cinnamon
3/4 cup (175 mL) unsalted butter, softened
1 cup (250 mL) sugar
2 eggs
1/2 tsp (2 mL) vanilla extract

Preheat the oven to 350°F (180°C).

Spread the Brazil nuts on one baking sheet and the almonds on another; toast until just golden, 5 to 8 minutes. (Toast them on 2 baking sheets because one kind of nut might take longer than the other.) Let cool, then transfer to a large bowl. Mix in the dates, cherries, pineapple and half of the flour.

In a separate bowl, stir together the remaining flour, baking soda, salt and cinnamon. In another bowl, beat together the butter and sugar until light and fluffy. Beat in the eggs and vanilla; continue beating to blend. Stir in the flour mixture. Using hands, mix in the dried fruit mixture until combined. Drop the dough by teaspoonfuls (10 mL) onto buttered or parchment paper–lined cookie sheets. Bake until slightly golden, 10 to 12 minutes.

Hazelnut Sandwich Cookies with Caramel

Hazelnuts and caramel are a match made in heaven. When we put these special cookies on our menu, our staff loved them as much as our customers. To gild the lily, you could add a layer of chocolate ganache, then the caramel filling. I like serving the cookies with tea for a treat in the afternoon, or for dessert as part of a cookie platter, along with fresh fruit or ice cream.

Makes about 20 sandwich cookies

Cookies:
1 cup (250 mL) butter
2/3 cup (150 mL) packed brown sugar
2 cups (500 mL) all-purpose flour
1 1/2 cups (375 mL) very finely chopped hazelnuts
Icing sugar

Caramel Filling:
1/3 cup (75 mL) butter
3/4 cup (175 mL) packed brown sugar
1/2 cup (125 mL) brandy
1/3 cup (75 mL) heavy cream
2 tbsp (30 mL) golden syrup

Preheat the oven to 325°F (160°C).

Cookies: In the bowl of an electric mixer, beat the butter and sugar until light and creamy. Add the flour and mix until combined. Place the nuts on a plate. One teaspoonful (5 mL) at a time, form dough into balls; drop each into the nuts and flatten, pressing nuts into one side and turning to press nuts into other side. Lift carefully onto a baking sheet and flatten into 2-inch (5 cm) diameter. Refrigerate for 10 to 15 minutes.

Bake until golden, 12 to 15 minutes, watching carefully that cookies don't get too brown. Transfer to a wire rack to let cool.

Caramel Filling: In a saucepan over low heat, mix together the butter, sugar, brandy, cream and golden syrup until smooth; simmer until slightly thickened, about 10 minutes. Refrigerate until cooled and just beginning to firm. Spread over half of the biscuits; sandwich with remaining biscuits. Dust with icing sugar.

G.B. Chocolate Brownies

This recipe is dedicated to and named for my stepdaughter, Gillian, who adores just about anything chocolate and loves to volunteer to make these. A warning does come with this recipe: they're very rich and should be cut into small squares so as not to cause chocolate overdose!

Makes about 20 squares

1 1/4 cups (300 mL) unsalted butter
1 1/2 cups (375 mL) sugar
5 eggs
1/2 tsp (2 mL) vanilla extract
1 cup (250 mL) Dutch-process cocoa powder
1 cup (250 mL) all-purpose flour
1/2 tsp (2 mL) sea salt
Dutch-process cocoa powder for dusting (optional)

Preheat the oven to 325°F (160°C).

In a saucepan, melt the butter over low heat. Add the sugar and cook, whisking constantly, until dissolved. Remove from heat and let cool before whisking in the eggs and vanilla. In a bowl, sift together the cocoa, flour and salt; stir into the butter mixture until just combined.

Pour into a buttered 9-inch (23 cm) square cake pan and bake until just set in the middle and slightly dry around edges only (do not overbake), about 15 minutes. Let cool completely. Dust with cocoa powder, if desired. Cut into 2-inch (2.5 cm) squares.

VARIATIONS
Gillian is a purist and won't consider adulterating this recipe with nuts or dried fruit, but I think scattering 1/2 cup (125 mL) chopped toasted hazelnuts or toasted pecans across the top before baking makes them even better. For a simple but fabulous finish to dinner, serve these with coffee ice cream dusted with cocoa powder.

Benjamin Bars

These bars are very close to my heart as they're named after the first child of one of our pastry chefs. In the kitchen, they're known fondly as Benny Bars. They include many of our favourite things, like dried cherries, chocolate and pecans. How can you go wrong?

Makes 20 bars

1 lb (500 g) unsalted butter
3 1/4 cups (800 mL) packed golden brown sugar
4 large eggs, free-range if possible
1 tbsp (15 mL) vanilla extract
2 1/2 cups (625 mL) all-purpose flour
4 tbsp (60 mL) espresso powder
1 tbsp (15 mL) baking soda
1/2 tsp (2 mL) sea salt
1 1/2 cups (375 mL) old-fashioned rolled oats
1 1/4 cups (300 mL) unsweetened flaked coconut
3 cups (750 mL) pecans, toasted
3 1/2 cups (875 mL) semi-sweet chocolate chips (I like to use Belgian chocolate)
3 cups (750 mL) dried tart cherries
Icing sugar

Preheat the oven to 350°F (180°C).

In a saucepan, melt the butter and sugar over low heat, stirring, until sugar is dissolved. Remove from heat and let cool. Beat in eggs and vanilla until glossy. In a separate bowl, sift together the flour, espresso powder, baking soda and salt. Stir in the oats, coconut, pecans, chocolate chips and dried cherries. Stir the oats mixture into the butter mixture.

Lightly butter a 13- x 9-inch (3 L) baking pan. Pour in the batter and spread evenly. Bake until edges pull away from sides, about 35 minutes. Let cool. Cut into 20 squares. Dust with icing sugar.

Belgian Chocolate and Dried Cherry Scones

Chunks of molten chocolate and tart dried cherries stud these scones. Sometimes I even serve these for dessert, cutting them into heart or star shapes, slicing them in half horizontally and filling them with fresh berries and whipped cream. They're also yummy served with berry coulis or chocolate sauce on the side.

Makes 18 to 20 scones

1 1/2 cups (375 mL) all-purpose flour
2 1/4 tsp (11 mL) baking powder
2 tsp (10 mL) sugar
1 1/2 tsp (7 mL) sea salt
6 tbsp (90 mL) cold butter, cut into 1/2-inch (1 cm) cubes
1/4 lb (125 g) sweet chocolate, cut into 1/2-inch (1 cm) chunks
1/4 lb (125 g) dried cherries
3/4 cup (175 mL) buttermilk
1 egg, beaten

Preheat the oven to 400°F (200°C). Lightly butter a cookie sheet, or line it with parchment paper.

In a large bowl, sift together the flour, baking powder, sugar and salt. Using fingers, work in the butter until the mixture is the texture of coarse sand. Toss in the chocolate and dried cherries. Pour in the buttermilk and stir until just combined.

Turn out the dough onto a lightly floured work surface. Roll out to 1-inch (2.5 cm) thickness. Cut out 2-inch (5 cm) rounds. Place scones on the prepared cookie sheet; brush tops with beaten egg. Bake until slightly golden, 10 to 12 minutes.

Strawberry Rhubarb Oatmeal Crisp

I'm a sucker for cobblers and crisps – homey, comforting desserts that remind me of growing up. My mother often made these types of desserts for our family, although this crisp puts a spin on the traditional version with pepper added to the fruit. You can also add fresh mint or candied ginger. Once you have the basic recipe down, let your imagination run wild.

Makes 6 to 8 servings

3 cups (750 mL) rhubarb cut into 1/2-inch (1 cm) pieces
2 cups (500 mL) fresh strawberries, stemmed and halved
3/4 cup (175 mL) sugar
1 tbsp (15 mL) freshly squeezed orange juice
1 tbsp (15 mL) cornstarch
1 tsp (5 mL) vanilla extract
1/4 tsp (1 mL) freshly ground pepper

Topping:
1 1/2 cups (375 mL) old-fashioned rolled oats
1 cup (250 mL) all-purpose flour
1 cup (250 mL) packed golden brown sugar
1 cup (250 mL) unsalted butter, cold, cut into cubes

Preheat the oven to 350°F (180°C).

In a large bowl, mix together the rhubarb, strawberries, sugar, orange juice, cornstarch, vanilla and pepper. Pour into a 10-inch (25 cm) baking dish with high sides.

Topping: In a bowl, combine the oats, flour and brown sugar. With your fingertips, work the butter into the mixture until texture is moist and mealy. Sprinkle on top of the fruit.

Bake until the fruit is bubbling and the topping is golden brown, 40 to 45 minutes.

Lemon Ginger Cobbler with Honey Nectarines

This cobbler is best served when nectarines are at their peak, in the late summer. It's perfect after a feast of ribs and corn. Serve with vanilla ice cream or crème fraîche.

Makes 6 to 8 servings

1 1/2 cups (375 mL) plus 2 tsp (10 mL) all-purpose flour
2 tbsp (30 mL) sugar
1 tsp (5 mL) baking powder
1/4 tsp (1 mL) sea salt
6 tbsp (90 mL) cold unsalted butter, cut into 1-inch (2.5 cm) chunks
2 tbsp (30 mL) chopped candied ginger
2 tsp (10 mL) grated lemon zest
2/3 cup (150 mL) chilled heavy cream
4 cups (1 L) nectarines, cut into 1/2-inch (1 cm) slices
2 tbsp (30 mL) liquid honey
2 tsp (10 mL) fresh lemon juice
1 egg, beaten
Coarse sugar (optional)

Preheat the oven 350°F (180°C).

In a bowl, sift together 1 1/2 cups (375 mL) flour, sugar, baking powder and salt. Cut in the butter until the mixture resembles coarse cornmeal. Add the ginger and lemon zest. Gradually add the cream, mixing until it just comes together.

Turn out onto a lightly floured work surface. Roll out to 1-inch (2.5 cm) thickness. Using the bottom of a glass or cookie cutter, cut the dough into 2 1/2-inch (6 cm) rounds. Set aside.

Slice the nectarines into a bowl. Gently mix in the honey and lemon juice. Sprinkle with the remaining 2 tsp (10 mL) flour. Spread the mixture in an oval or rectangular baking dish about 9 inches (23 cm) across. Place the cobbler rounds on top of the nectarines; brush with the beaten egg and sprinkle with coarse sugar, if desired.

Bake until the nectarines are bubbling and the cobbler top is light golden, 30 to 40 minutes.

Caramelized Apple and Rosemary Bread Pudding

As a member of Les Dames d'Escoffier, I'm often called upon to participate in events to raise funds for scholarships and outreach programs in the community. This recipe was developed for a food and wine grazing event in Vancouver. To say it was a hit would be an understatement. I think most people were drawn to the comforting quality of this dessert and the interesting combination of rosemary, apple and ginger. Actually, the pairing of rosemary and apples comes from medieval times, when savoury and sweet often crossed over.

Makes 6 to 8 servings

1⁄4 cup (50 mL) butter
3⁄4 cup (175 mL) plus 4 tbsp (60 mL) sugar
4 apples, peeled, cored and cut into 1-inch (2.5 cm) chunks
5 cups (1.25 L) light cream
1/3 cup (75 mL) liquid honey
6 eggs
2 tsp (10 mL) vanilla extract
6 slices (1/2 inch/1 cm thick) challah, cut into 2-inch (5 cm) cubes
1⁄4 cup (50 mL) chopped candied ginger
1 tsp (5 mL) chopped fresh rosemary
Crème fraîche (page 25)
Caramel sauce (page 179)

Preheat the oven to 350°F (180°C).

In a large sauté pan, melt the butter over medium heat; cook 3⁄4 cup (175 mL) sugar until it starts to brown. Stir in the apples. The caramel will immediately harden but will melt again. Cook until apples are slightly softened and caramelized. Remove from heat and let cool.

Meanwhile, in a bowl, beat together the cream, honey, remaining 4 tbsp (60 mL) sugar, eggs and vanilla until combined. Spread the bread cubes in a gratin dish and scatter the caramel apples, candied ginger and rosemary over top. Pour the egg mixture over the bread and apples. Bake for about 45 minutes.

Serve warm with crème fraîche and caramel sauce.

Apple Caramel Crostata with Red Wine Caramel

In an era of highly processed food, we're lucky that many farmers are taking a stand and working hard to develop and nurture heirloom varieties of fruit and vegetables. The apple varieties available are growing each year, and I strongly urge you to try some. In this contemporary version of apple pie, you can use Bramley, Jonathan, Golden Delicious, Rome Beauty or your favourite locally harvested cooking apple.

Makes 6 to 8 servings

1/2 batch Food Processor Tart Dough (page 155)
1 1/2 lb (750 g) Gala or Granny Smith apples (about 4 average apples)
4 tbsp (60 mL) unsalted butter
1/2 cup (125 mL) sugar
1/2 cup (125 mL) red wine

Preheat the oven to 400°F (200°C).

On a lightly floured surface, roll out the dough into an 11-inch (28 cm) circle; transfer to a baking sheet. Peel and core apples; cut into thin wedges.

In a large cast-iron skillet over medium heat, melt the butter; add the sugar, which will slowly melt. Reduce heat and cook while the sugar mixture gradually darkens to a rich mahogany colour. This can take 10 to 15 minutes. (Do not stir; you can swirl the pan as it starts to turn golden, to keep it uniform.)

Add the apples to the caramel. The caramel will immediately harden, then slowly melt again. Cook, turning to coat apples with caramel, for about 10 minutes. Remove apples from caramel and let cool completely. Add wine to remaining caramel in pan; bring to a boil, then reduce heat and simmer until the caramel coats the back of a spoon.

Pile the caramel-coated apple chunks in the centre of the dough, leaving a 1 1/2-inch (3.5 cm) border around the outside edge. Raise the dough border to enclose the sides of the tart, letting it drape gently over the fruit. Bake until the crust is golden and the apples are soft, about 25 minutes, checking the tart halfway through baking to prevent burning. If the crust is browning too fast, cover with foil. Let cool on a rack for 10 minutes. Serve warm with the red wine caramel sauce.

Food Processor Tart Dough

This recipe will make enough dough to line two 9-inch (23 cm) pie plates or to make one double-crust pie. If only using half the recipe, freeze the remaining. For best results, use very cold butter.

1/2 lb (250 g) cold unsalted butter
2 cups (500 mL) unbleached all-purpose flour
1/4 cup (50 mL) sugar
1/2 tsp (2 mL) sea salt
1/4 cup (50 mL) ice water

Cut the butter into 1/2-inch (1 cm) cubes. Since butter softens rapidly with handling, return the cubes to the refrigerator for at least 10 minutes while continuing with next step.

In a food processor fitted with a steel blade, combine the flour, sugar and salt; pulse a few times to mix. Add the butter, tossing quickly with your fingers to coat each cube with flour, taking care not to touch the blade. This prevents the butter cubes from sticking together and helps them break apart and combine more evenly with the flour. Pulse about 15 times or until the butter particles are the size of small peas.

With the motor running, add the ice water all at once through the feed tube. Process for about 10 seconds, stopping the machine before the dough becomes a solid mass.

Turn out the dough onto a sheet of foil, pressing any loose particles into the mass. Roughly form into a 7-inch (18 cm) disc. Cover completely with foil and refrigerate for at least 1 hour. The dough can be refrigerated for up to 2 days or frozen for up to 2 weeks.

To blind bake: Preheat the oven to 350°F (180°C). Line a pie dish with the pastry and cover with foil or parchment paper. Fill the shell with dried beans, rice or baking weights. Bake until light golden brown, 20 to 25 minutes. If you wish to brown the inside of the shell, remove the foil and weights after 10 minutes and return to the oven for the remaining 10 to 15 minutes.

Chocolate Pistachio Pear Tart with Chocolate Drizzle

At LSFF, our approach to pastry is to take the art and technique that the French have mastered so well and tailor it to North American tastes. This particular tart evolved from that philosophy. In almost every pastry shop in Paris, you'll find pear tarts with almond frangipane; we decided to replace the almonds with pistachios and stud the tart with chunks of Belgian chocolate. For best results, make sure the pastry shell is completely cooked on the bottom before you add the pears and frangipane filling. Also, watch that the edge of the pastry doesn't brown too much; if necessary, you can prevent this by covering it with a strip of foil halfway through baking.

Makes 8 servings

1 tart shell (9 inches/23 cm), baked (see Food Processor Tart Dough, page 155)
4 ripe pears, peeled, cored and halved
3 oz (90 g) best-quality semi-sweet chocolate, chopped
Vanilla ice cream

Pistachio Frangipane:
1/2 cup (125 mL) unsalted butter, softened
1/2 cup (125 mL) icing sugar
2 eggs
1/2 cup (125 mL) pistachios, ground
2 tbsp (30 mL) all-purpose flour

Chocolate Drizzle:
1/2 cup (125 mL) heavy cream
6 oz (180 g) best-quality bittersweet chocolate, chopped

Preheat the oven to 350°F (180°C).

Pistachio Frangipane: In a food processor, combine the butter, icing sugar, eggs, pistachios and flour; process until smooth. Spread over the base of the tart shell.

Slice the pear halves crosswise 1/4 inch (5 mm) thick, cutting almost but not all the way through, keeping the slices together so the pear halves retain their shape. Fanning slightly, arrange pear halves over frangipane with the narrow end facing inward. Press pieces of chocolate into frangipane.

Bake until set, about 40 minutes. If the exposed pastry edges are becoming too brown, remove from oven and cover with strips of foil. Continue baking.

Chocolate Drizzle: In a saucepan, heat the heavy cream until it just starts to bubble. Add the chocolate. Remove from heat and let stand until the chocolate is melted, 3 to 4 minutes. Whisk until smooth.

Pour a little of the Chocolate Drizzle on each plate and arrange a tart slice on top. Serve warm or at room temperature with a scoop of vanilla ice cream on the side.

Chocolate Mocha Pots de Crème

Calling all chocoholics! This one's for you. Creamy rich with a real chocolate hit, a small portion is all you need to satisfy that craving for good chocolate. This recipe multiplies well and can be made the day before serving.

Makes 8 servings

6 oz (180 g) best-quality bittersweet chocolate, finely chopped
4 cups (1 L) heavy cream
1 tbsp (15 mL) brewed dark-roast coffee
Pinch sea salt
6 egg yolks, preferably free-range
1/2 cup (125 mL) packed golden brown sugar
Softly whipped cream (optional)

Preheat the oven to 325°F (160°C).

In a heavy saucepan, heat the chocolate, cream, coffee and salt over low heat until chocolate melts. Remove from heat and whisk until smooth. Set aside to let cool slightly. In a bowl, whisk together the egg yolks and sugar. Gradually whisk the warm chocolate cream into the egg mixture.

Strain into eight 4- or 5-oz (125 or 150 mL) ramekins. Place the ramekins in a large ovenproof dish. Carefully pour enough hot water into pan to come halfway up the side of the ramekins. Carefully place in the oven and bake until set but still jiggly in the centre, about 45 minutes. Remove ramekins from water bath and refrigerate for at least 2 hours or until chilled or for up to 48 hours. Serve with softly whipped cream, if desired.

Lemon Almond Dacquoise

This recipe is a classic, and has been on our menu since we first started creating desserts. Light, crunchy and lemony, it satisfies the pickiest sweet tooth. In the summer, we cover the Lemon Curd with a layer of fresh blueberries, raspberries or black-berries; use your imagination.

Makes 8 servings

1/3 cup (75 mL) whole almonds
1 cup (250 mL) sugar
4 egg whites at room temperature
1 cup (250 mL) heavy cream, whipped
Icing sugar
8 pieces grated lemon zest
8 small sprigs fresh mint

Lemon Curd:
1/2 cup (125 mL) butter
1/2 cup (125 mL) sugar
Grated zest and juice of 2 lemons
4 eggs yolks, beaten and strained

Preheat the oven to 250°F (120°C).

Lemon Curd: In a heavy non-aluminum pan over low heat, melt the but-ter and sugar until the sugar is completely dissolved. Remove from heat and add the lemon zest and juice, and eggs. Return to heat and cook, stirring constantly, until mixture thickens, being careful not to overcook. Refrigerate to chill completely before using.

Place the almonds in a small saucepan and cover with water; bring to a boil. Remove from heat and let stand for 10 minutes; drain and pat dry. In a food processor, grind the almonds and 1/2 cup (125 mL) of the sugar until the mixture is fairly fine but not a paste. Whisk the egg whites until soft peaks form; gradually whisk in the remaining sugar. Fold the almond mixture into the meringue.

Spoon the meringue mixture onto a 13- x 9-inch (3 L) parchment paper–lined baking pan. Spread out to form 2 rectangular shapes, each about 12 x 4 inches (30 x 10 cm). Bake for 1 hour. Turn off oven and let meringues stand in oven for another hour. Remove from the oven and let cool completely.

Place 1 of the meringues on a serving platter and cover with two-thirds of the Lemon Curd. Cover with 1 cup (250 mL) of the whipped cream. Spread the remaining Lemon Curd over cream. Top with second meringue. Dust with icing sugar and decorate with lemon zest and mint leaves.

Demystifying Meringue

Lemon Almond Dacquoise was one of our most requested desserts – a close second after everything chocolate. Not only is it delicious and light but it's also a recipe many people are afraid to attempt on their own. It really isn't that difficult; you just have to follow a few rules, and success will be yours.

Make sure your bowl and mixer are free of any traces of oil or fat.

Ensure the egg whites are at room temperature and are as fresh as possible. The meringue will be more stable if the whites are fresh.

Pay close attention to the whites when beating them; you want to add the sugar at the soft peak stage. If you wait too long, the meringue gets dry and breaks up.

I like to turn the oven off once the meringue is baked and leave it inside while the oven cools. That way, there's a bit less cracking, and it has more of a chance to dry out.

White Chocolate Pecan Dream

Even those of you who are not enamoured of white chocolate will dive into this dessert. It's light, not too sweet, cuts like a dream and freezes beautifully. Although I'm not a great advocate of the freezer, I know everyone is pressed for time, so if it means you might try this dessert if you could make it a few days in advance, then I'm all for it. When making desserts, you want to enjoy yourself, so set aside the time. When the children have gone to bed, turn on the CD player, heat up the oven and go for it.

Makes 8 generous servings

3/4 cup (175 mL) all-purpose flour
1/2 cup (125 mL) sugar
1/4 cup (50 mL) pecans, finely ground
1/2 tsp (2 mL) baking soda
1/4 tsp (1 mL) sea salt
1/2 cup (125 mL) freshly squeezed orange juice
1/4 cup (50 mL) canola oil
1 tbsp (15 mL) white vinegar
1 1/2 cups (375 mL) fresh raspberries, blueberries, blackberries
    or small strawberries
OR 2 cups (500 mL) white chocolate curls
    (see Making Chocolate Curls, page 161)
Icing sugar

Filling:
12 oz (375 g) white chocolate
3/4 cup (175 mL) plus 1 1/2 cups (375 mL) heavy cream
1 1/2 tsp (7 mL) gelatin
3 tbsp (45 mL) cold water
1/2 cup (125 mL) pecans, chopped and toasted

Preheat the oven to 350°F (180°C). Butter a 9-inch (2.5 L) springform pan and line it with parchment paper.

In a bowl, combine the flour, sugar, pecans, baking soda and salt. In another bowl, mix together the orange juice, oil and vinegar; pour into the dry ingredients and mix until well blended. Pour into the prepared pan. Bake until a skewer inserted in the cake comes out clean, 15 to 20 minutes. Let cool to room temperature.

Filling: In a small heavy-bottomed saucepan over low heat, warm the chocolate and 3/4 cup (175 mL) cream, stirring constantly, until the chocolate is completely melted. Remove from heat.

In a small bowl, dissolve the gelatin in the cold water; stir into the chocolate cream while it's still hot. Let cool to room temperature and stir in the pecans. Whip 1 1/2 cups (375 mL) cream till soft peaks form; fold into chocolate cream mixture. Pour over cake base and refrigerate for at least 4 hours or overnight. The cake can be wrapped and frozen for up to 2 weeks. Let thaw before continuing.

Run a knife between the cake and the pan to loosen. Unclip the ring and carefully transfer the cake to a serving platter. Garnish with fresh berries or white chocolate curls and dust with icing sugar. Keep cake refrigerated until serving.

Making Chocolate Curls

Chocolate curls are the best of both worlds – pretty and delicious. They're easy to make. Use different kinds of chocolate for different results and visual effects. White chocolate, milk chocolate and dark chocolate all work well.

1 lb (500 g) block chocolate (Callebaut or Valrhona)

In a microwave set to defrost, soften the block of chocolate for 15 seconds. (Dark chocolate will likely take a little longer to soften than white.) Using a vegetable peeler, peel off strips of chocolate, gently lifting onto a platter or baking sheet. (You may need to soften the block in the microwave more than once, but be careful not to melt it.) Use the heel of your hand to continue softening chocolate between removing strips. If it's warm in your kitchen, refrigerate the curls as you go – they lose their shape quickly.

Espresso Pannacotta with Espresso Chocolate Sauce

Pannacotta is one of my standbys. An Italian classic, the name translates as "cooked cream." There are so many variations, depending on the season and the rest of your menu. Lemon, lime, lavender, vanilla, orange, anise, almond – use your imagination. I like this pairing of chocolate and coffee, just right to finish a meal. By now you may realize I have a serious chocolate problem, but can you blame me? With so much good-quality chocolate readily available, it's hard to resist.

Makes 6 servings

1 tbsp (15 mL) gelatin
2 tbsp (30 mL) water
3 cups (750 mL) heavy cream
2/3 cup (150 mL) icing sugar
3 tbsp (45 mL) brewed espresso
1/2 vanilla bean, split lengthwise
Espresso Chocolate Sauce (recipe follows)

In a small bowl, soften the gelatin in the water; set aside. In a saucepan over medium-high heat, combine the cream, icing sugar, espresso and vanilla bean; bring to a boil, then remove from heat. Remove the vanilla bean and stir in the gelatin until dissolved.

Pour the mixture into 6 ramekins. Refrigerate for at least 2 hours or until chilled. To unmould, run a hot knife around the inside of each ramekin and turn out onto individual plates. Serve with Espresso Chocolate Sauce.

Espresso Chocolate Sauce

4 oz (125 g) semi-sweet chocolate, chopped
1/4 cup (50 mL) unsalted butter
1/4 cup (50 mL) corn syrup
1 tbsp (15 mL) espresso powder
1/4 cup (50 mL) heavy cream

In a small heavy saucepan, combine the chocolate, butter, corn syrup and espresso powder. Heat slowly, stirring occasionally, until melted and blended. Remove from heat and stir in the cream.

Figs Poached in Chianti with Zabaglione

This is a fabulous dessert for the end of summer and can be made well into the fall using dried Calimyrna or Turkish figs. When using dried figs, you have to poach them longer than fresh figs, 20 to 30 minutes to soften. Zabaglione must not be cooked over direct heat or it will curdle; use a double boiler.

Makes 6 servings

2 cups (500 mL) Chianti or other dry red wine
1 cup (250 mL) water
1/2 cup (125 mL) sugar
18 fresh figs

Zabaglione:
4 egg yolks
1/4 cup (50 mL) sugar
1/2 cup (125 mL) Marsala

In a small deep saucepan, heat the wine, water and sugar until sugar is dissolved. Add the whole figs. Cover with a piece of parchment paper and a lid. Simmer gently for 10 to 15 minutes. Remove from heat. Let the figs cool in the liquid. Remove the figs and return the wine to the heat; simmer until liquid reaches the consistency of syrup.

Zabaglione: In the top of a double boiler, combine the egg yolks and sugar and whisk until yellow and creamy. In the bottom of a double boiler, bring water to the brink of a simmer (do not boil). Place the egg mixture over the water. Add Marsala and continue whisking until mixture foams and swells into a light, soft mass, then forms soft mounds. Remove from heat when soft mounds form.

Spoon some of the reduced wine syrup onto each of 6 plates. Place three figs on top of each. Spoon the zabaglione on top and serve immediately.

Chocolate Phyllo Purses
with Late-Harvest Sémillon Sabayon

Phyllo pastry became a staple in our kitchen in the 1980s and has been there ever since. Once you feel confident with it, you'll appreciate its versatility. The key is to keep a damp cloth over the phyllo you aren't working with. You can't leave it sitting uncovered for more than a couple of minutes or it starts to dry out and crumble. The chocolate phyllo purses require only a few ingredients. For other sexy, impressive variations, serve them with a berry coulis or crème fraîche or ice cream instead of the sabayon. A note to all single men out there: here's a dessert you can master and you'll have dinner dates lining up.

Makes 6 servings

18 7 x 7-inch (18 x 18 cm) squares of phyllo pastry, cut from full-size phyllo sheets
3/4 cup (175 mL) melted unsalted butter
6 tbsp (90 mL) sugar
6 oz (180 g) semi-sweet Belgian chocolate, finely chopped
Late-Harvest Sémillon Sabayon (recipe follows)
Dutch-process cocoa powder

Preheat the oven to 350°F (180°C).

Lay 1 phyllo pastry square on a flat, dry surface and brush lightly with melted butter. Sprinkle with some of the sugar. Cover with another phyllo square and repeat brushing with butter and sprinkling with sugar. Cover with a third phyllo square. Spoon about 1 oz (30 g) of the chocolate in the centre. Gather up phyllo like a little purse and pinch together just above the chocolate. Brush with butter and sprinkle with a little more sugar. Keep refrigerated until ready to bake. Repeat to make 5 more phyllo purses. Bake until the phyllo is golden brown, about 15 minutes.

Spoon some of the Late-Harvest Sémillon Sabayon onto each of 6 dessert plates; place a warm phyllo purse on top. Dust with cocoa powder to serve.

You can serve this sabayon with almost any kind of fruit for a showy dessert. If you can't find late-harvest Sémillon, use another kind of dessert wine, such as icewine. The flavour will vary with the choice of wine.

Late-Harvest Sémillon Sabayon

Makes 6 servings

6 egg yolks
1/2 cup (125 mL) late-harvest Sémillon
1/3 cup (75 mL) sugar
1/8 tsp (0.5 mL) sea salt
1/2 cup (125 mL) heavy cream, whipped

In the top of a double boiler, beat together the egg yolks, wine, sugar and salt, whisking constantly until thickened, 5 to 10 minutes. Remove from heat. Place the top of the double boiler in a larger bowl of ice water and continue whisking until cool. Fold in cream. Can be cooled, covered and refrigerated for up to 8 hours.

Quick Tempering Method for Chocolate

Chop 1 lb (500 g) chocolate into very small pieces and set aside one-third. Melt remaining two-thirds in the top of a double boiler over hot, but not simmering, water, stirring frequently with a rubber spatula to ensure even melting. The chocolate should not exceed 120°F (50°C) (110°F/45°C for white chocolate) or it will burn. Remove the double boiler from heat; remove the top pan of the double boiler and wipe it dry. Stir in the remaining chocolate in 3 batches, making sure each is completely melted before adding the next. When all of the pieces have been added, the chocolate will be tempered. Perfect for dipping strawberries!

Crispy Sugared Won Ton Leaves with Pumpkin Cream and Maple Syrup

While it may sound involved, this dessert is pretty simple, although it does require some last-minute assembly. I created it for a formal fall dinner focused on seasonal flavours. I love to give a new twist to common ingredients. Combining pumpkin and won tons is unusual, but it works well.

Makes 6 servings

1 cup (250 mL) pumpkin purée (not sweetened pie filling)
4 tbsp (60 mL) maple syrup plus 2 tbsp (30 mL) for garnish
1/4 tsp (1 mL) cinnamon
1/8 tsp (0.5 mL) freshly grated nutmeg
1/8 tsp (0.5 mL) allspice
1 1/2 cups (375 mL) heavy cream
18 won ton wrappers
6 tbsp (90 mL) melted unsalted butter
Sugar
Icing sugar

Preheat the oven to 350°F (180°C).

In a bowl, blend together the pumpkin purée, 4 tbsp (60 mL) maple syrup, cinnamon, nutmeg and allspice until smooth. Whip the cream until soft peaks form; fold gently into the pumpkin purée. Refrigerate.

Brush both sides of the won ton wrappers with butter and sprinkle both sides lightly with sugar. Place on a cookie sheet and bake until crispy and golden, about 10 minutes. Let cool.

Drizzle each of 6 dessert plates with some of the remaining 2 tbsp (30 mL) maple syrup. Place a won ton wrapper in the centre of each plate. Spoon about 2 tbsp (30 mL) of the pumpkin cream in the centre and cover with another won ton wrapper and filling. Top with a third wrapper to create a little stack of 3 wrappers and filling. Dust the tops with icing sugar and serve immediately.

Candied Ginger and Macadamia Nut Ice Cream

Buying an ice cream maker is worth the investment since there's nothing quite like fresh-churned ice cream. The flavour combinations are endless; this one is especially sublime. Try serving it with thick slices of bananas warmed in a little caramel sauce. Yum.

Makes 8 servings

4 egg yolks
3/4 cup (175 mL) sugar
1/8 tsp (0.5 mL) sea salt
1 1/2 cups (375 mL) milk
4 tsp (20 mL) vanilla extract
2 inches (5 cm) vanilla bean, split lengthwise
3 cups (750 mL) heavy cream
1 cup (250 mL) coarsely chopped toasted macadamia nuts
1/2 cup (125 mL) candied ginger, coarsely chopped

In a bowl, whisk together the egg yolks, sugar and salt.

Meanwhile, in a saucepan, bring the milk to the boiling point; mix in vanilla extract. Scrape seeds from vanilla bean halves into milk; drop in bean. Mix into the egg mixture, then pour back into the pan. Heat gently, stirring constantly, until the custard is thick enough to lightly coat a wooden spatula or a spoon. Remove from heat and refrigerate until cold, about 2 hours. Remove bean.

Stir the heavy cream into the custard. Pour into an ice cream maker and freeze according to manufacturer's instructions until partially frozen. Add macadamia nuts and candied ginger and stir until evenly distributed. Continue freezing until set.

Death by Chocolate with Raspberry Splash

To many, this dessert needs no introduction, as it was our signature dessert for years. The story goes like this: When I decided to take the plunge and open my own catering operation in 1985, I knew we couldn't rely on fluctuating seasonal business to keep the doors open. I saw a real need for a company that could provide top-quality desserts to high-end restaurants that didn't have their own pastry chefs. One of the first restaurants I approached was Bishop's, which had also recently opened. John Bishop was interested, as long as we would make desserts that were exclusive to him. In walked Death by Chocolate. Of course, in hindsight we should have trademarked the name. Today, there's even a chain of dessert restaurants named Death by Chocolate. I do give John credit for having the inspired idea of putting the dessert plate in a large cardboard box and then splashing the raspberry coulis on the plate before laying the slice of Death by Chocolate on top. Needless to say, this created a very dramatic effect. At one time, Death by Chocolate even had the honour of being Prime Minister Pierre Trudeau's favourite dessert. He often ordered more than one piece when he was at Bishop's. Now, after all these years of fielding requests for this recipe, I've decided to share it here. As you see, it makes a lot; however, it does freeze well, so you'll just have to throw another dinner party.

Makes 16 servings

15 oz (450 g) best-quality bittersweet chocolate (Valrhona or Callebaut work well)
1 cup (250 mL) heavy cream
4 tbsp (60 mL) butter
4 egg yolks
1/2 cup (125 mL) icing sugar
6 tbsp (90 mL) Cointreau or Grand Marnier
Cocoa powder for dusting

Raspberry Splash:
10 oz (300 g) frozen raspberries
3 tbsp (45 mL) berry sugar
1 tsp (5 mL) fresh lemon juice

Line a 9- by 5-inch (2 L) loaf pan with parchment paper.

Chop the chocolate into small pieces and place in the top of a double boiler; add the cream and butter. Melt over medium heat, stirring until completely smooth. Remove from heat and let cool for 1 minute, continuing to stir.

Whisk in the egg yolks. Sift the icing sugar into the chocolate mixture, whisking constantly. Whisk in the Cointreau until smooth. Pour into the prepared pan. Refrigerate for at least 8 hours to set or overnight.

Raspberry Splash: In a food processor, purée the raspberries, berry sugar and lemon juice. Pass the sauce through a sieve to remove the seeds.

Unmould the cake, removing paper. Dust the top with cocoa powder. Drizzle a large spoonful of Raspberry Splash on each plate. Using a hot, wet knife, slice cake and place on plates.

Wobbly Wedding Cakes

At LSFF, we were always known for our spectacular wedding cakes, and we worked hard to stay ahead of the curve, in terms of not only design but also flavour. I've even received phone calls from couples who've been married for years, telling me how much they loved their wedding cake. Our favourite part was designing, baking and decorating them. Transporting them, on the other hand, was another story, always the most difficult and nerve-wracking part.

One of the first cakes I made was for my father's boss's daughter – gee, no pressure there! Actually, making the cake was a breeze; it was a three-tier, buttercream cake with a basket-weave finish, decorated with fresh flowers. Ever so carefully, I drove it over to the house where the reception was to take place and gingerly lifted it out of the van. But I failed to notice the garden hose that lay across the steps halfway up the path. No one was around to see the look of horror and panic on my face as I tripped, desperately trying to save the cake. It wasn't a total loss, but the repair job was fairly extensive. Luckily, I had allowed lots of time before the reception and managed to return with the cake before anyone noticed it was missing.

Our cakes have travelled far, including to Toronto, Halifax and the Napa Valley. But it wasn't these travelling cakes that were the biggest challenge; it was the towering creations that only needed to go across town or up to Whistler. What with summer heat, traffic jams and potholed roads, some of these jaunts were truly hair-raising. We considered every cake that arrived unscathed a small miracle. If brides only knew what it takes to get their cake to the reception, they would be amazed. Actually, it's probably best they don't know.

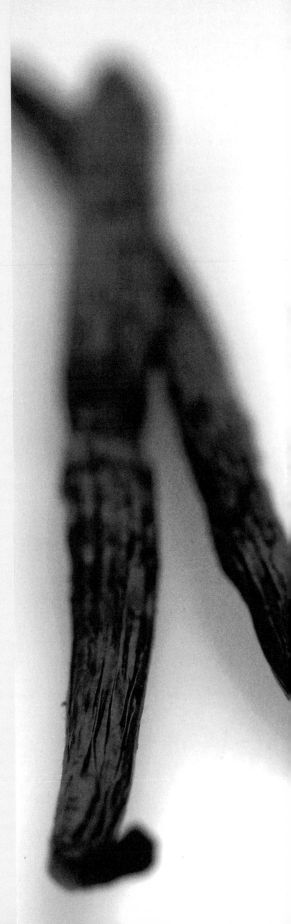

Crème Anglaise

Crème Anglaise should be a standard in everyone's dessert repertoire – an alternative to whipped cream or ice cream. It's especially good drizzled on bread puddings, pound cakes and cobblers. The basic recipe can be served as is or flavoured with mint, ginger, chocolate, cinnamon or citrus zest.

Makes 2 cups (500 mL)

2 cups (500 mL) light cream
1/2 vanilla bean, split lengthwise
5 egg yolks
1/3 cup (75 mL) sugar

In a small saucepan, heat the cream and vanilla bean over medium-low heat just until the cream starts to bubble around the edges. Remove from heat and let stand for 5 to 10 minutes.

In a bowl, whisk the egg yolks and sugar until pale yellow. Slowly whisk in the warm cream mixture. Place over low heat and cook gently, stirring constantly, until thickened enough to coat the back of a spoon. Do not let it come even close to a boil or you will have sweet scrambled eggs!

Remove from heat and immediately pour into a clean bowl. If you don't want to use it immediately, place the bowl in another bowl of ice water and stir until cool. Remove the vanilla bean and discard. Refrigerate until ready to use. Crème Anglaise will keep for up to 1 week.

Cinnamon Red Wine Sauce

Try serving this red wine sauce with fresh berries, poached fruit or ice cream. If you can't find arrowroot powder, substitute cornstarch.

Makes 1 1/2 cups (375 mL)

3 cups (750 mL) dry red wine
1 cup (250 mL) sugar
1 stick (4 inches/10 cm) cinnamon
1 tbsp (15 mL) arrowroot powder
1 tbsp (15 mL) water

In a heavy saucepan, stir together the wine and sugar. Add the cinnamon stick and bring to a boil. Reduce heat and simmer until reduced to 1 1/2 cups (375 mL). Mix arrowroot with water. Add to wine reduction. Return mixture to a boil. Remove from heat and strain. Use immediately or let cool and refrigerate for up to 10 days.

Chapter Eight

HOLIDAY GIFTS & RECIPES

The aroma of good food wafting through the house evokes warm memories of holiday celebrations. Spices, fruit, nuts and a fragrant ham help create a perfect holiday atmosphere.

For a number of years, we taught cooking classes in the autumn months leading up to the prime entertaining season. One of the most popular of these courses was making food gifts. These treats are ideal for hostesses, teachers, dog walkers, babysitters and all the people in your life you want to acknowledge in some way. The recipes here cover a broad spectrum: Vanilla Vinegar, which is amazing in vinaigrettes or in beurre blanc for steamed lobster; Caramel Sauce, which can be made in a moment and packaged with your favourite chocolate sauce for the sweet tooth on your list; and Seven-Day Preserved Lemons, which you can present along with a recipe. One of the keys to successful food gifts is the packaging. Look for interesting containers, creative labels and sumptuous ribbons to raise your gift giving to a whole new level.

Holiday foods are those traditional dishes that uphold the season's sense of tradition. I've given a few twists to the familiar holiday ham, filling it with a festive mixture of dried fruits and lacing it with bourbon. It could quickly become a favourite in your home. The Christmas Trifle with Marsala uses panettone instead of the traditional sponge cake and Marsala instead of sherry. And to get you through the "crazy season," as we at LSFF call it, the Cranberry Cosmopolitan will help keep you in a festive mood.

Spicy Apple Chutney

I used to think of chutney as one of those mysterious jars in the fridge, totally forgotten about, buried deeper and deeper until spring cleaning, when you decide you better throw it out because you've lost track of how long it's been there. Enter Spicy Apple Chutney. Whenever we run out, customers call to find out when we're making it again. It's great with roasted pork and tourtières, and in sandwiches with cheddar cheese and watercress. Or try it on a samosa for a terrific flavour combination.

Makes 12 cups (3 L)

1 tbsp (15 mL) vegetable oil
3 tbsp (45 mL) yellow mustard seeds
3 onions, diced
3 red bell peppers, diced
2 tbsp (30 mL) puréed garlic
1 tbsp (15 mL) chopped fresh gingerroot
3 jalapeño peppers, seeded and diced
1 tbsp (15 mL) allspice
3 cups (750 mL) sugar
3 cups (750 mL) water
2 cups (500 mL) white vinegar
6 pears, peeled, cored and diced
6 apples, peeled, cored and diced
3/4 cup (175 mL) golden raisins

In a large pot, heat the oil over medium heat; cook the mustard seeds, stirring, until they start to pop. Add the onions, red peppers, garlic, gingerroot, jalapeños and allspice; sauté until soft. Stir in the sugar, water, vinegar, pears, apples and raisins; mix well. Reduce heat to medium-low and cook until soft and thickened, 1 to 2 hours.

Remove from heat and let cool. Transfer to a food processor and purée in batches. Pour into clean jars and store in the refrigerator for up to 1 month.

Vanilla Vinegar

When Maggie Aro, one of the LSFF staff members, decided to honeymoon in Tahiti, we were the fortunate beneficiaries of some incredible vanilla beans she brought home. We set to work brewing this intoxicating creation. Use it to make a simple vinaigrette for a butter lettuce salad or a vanilla beurre blanc for seafood.

Makes 2 cups (500 mL)

2 cups (500 mL) champagne vinegar or white wine vinegar
1 vanilla bean, as fresh and plump as you can find

Split the vanilla bean lengthwise and scrape out the seeds. Reserve seeds for another use (they're great in vanilla sugar).

Pour the champagne vinegar into a wide-mouth container. Add the vanilla bean halves and mix well. Cover tightly and store in a cool, dark place for at least 2 weeks. Remove vanilla beans and transfer the liquid into a dark glass bottle with a tight-fitting lid. Vanilla vinegar will keep indefinitely in a cool, dark place.

Holiday Gifts It's often the case that the nicest gifts are handmade. Many of the recipes in this chapter would make a great present for a busy cook over the holidays. Use an attractive jar or tin box, add some raffia or ribbon, and make your own label to create a special, personal gift. If you like, package a holiday basket containing several little jars and containers.

Festive Olives and Cranberries

This smells like Christmas when you're making it. I love the look of the olives, kumquats and cranberries in glass clip jars tied with raffia.

Makes 4 pints (2 L)

1/4 cup (50 mL) extra-virgin olive oil
2 cloves garlic, crushed
7 dried hot chilies
3 cups (750 mL) imported black olives, packed in brine (not drained)
3 cups (750 mL) imported green olives, packed in brine (not drained)
1 cup (250 mL) fresh cranberries
1 cup (250 mL) kumquats, stems removed and sliced into
   1/4-inch (5 mm) thick rounds, seeds removed
1/2 cup (125 mL) fresh mint leaves

In a saucepan, heat the oil over low heat; cook the garlic and 3 of the chilies until garlic is golden. Remove from heat and let stand until flavours are infused, about 10 minutes. Discard garlic and chilies, reserving oil.

In a large bowl, gently stir together the black and green olives (with brine), cranberries, kumquats, mint and infused oil. Divide among four 1-pint (500 mL) sterilized jars, making sure that the olives are covered with liquid. Place one of the remaining chilies in each jar. Seal lids and refrigerate for at least 1 week. Can be stored in the refrigerator for up to 3 months. Let come to room temperature before serving.

Seven-Day Preserved Lemons

Ever since I started reading Paula Wolfert's cookbooks on Middle Eastern and Moroccan food, I've been making preserved lemons. As you see from the recipe, they're dead easy to make and so useful in all kinds of recipes. The problem is, if you come across a recipe that calls for them, you have to have them already made. So be prepared and have a jar handy to liven up soups, stews, seafood and veggie dishes.

Makes 16 pieces

2 lemons
1/3 cup (75 mL) coarse sea salt
1/2 cup (125 mL) fresh lemon juice
Olive oil

Scrub the lemons and dry well. Cut each into 8 wedges. Toss the wedges with the salt and place in a 2-pint (1 L) canning jar with a plastic-coated lid. Pour in the lemon juice and close the lid tightly. Let stand at room temperature for 7 days, shaking the jar each day to redistribute the salt and juice. To store, pour in enough olive oil to cover; refrigerate for up to 6 months.

To use, cut away the flesh of the lemon and discard. Chop the rind and use.

Caramel Sauce

You'll never buy caramel sauce again after you see how easy and fabulous this recipe is. Fruit desserts, bread puddings and ice cream will all be transformed into something better with a drizzle or spoonful of caramel sauce.

Makes 3/4 cup (175 mL)

1 cup (250 mL) sugar
1/3 cup (75 mL) water
1/2 cup (125 mL) heavy cream, warmed

In a heavy-bottomed saucepan, combine the sugar and water over low heat, stirring until sugar is dissolved. Increase heat to high and cook until sugar is golden amber.

Remove from heat and very slowly pour in the warm cream, stirring to combine. The caramel will bubble up as you add the cream, so add it slowly. Return to low heat if necessary, stirring until blended.

The sauce can be served immediately, or poured into a plastic container and refrigerated up to 2 weeks or frozen for up to 2 months.

Christmas Mandarin Orange Marmalade

If you give this as a holiday gift, you'll start a tradition. It's so pretty and delicious, your friends will be hoping to receive it every year. You may have to double the recipe to cover your entire gift list.

Makes 2 cups (500 mL)

3 mandarin oranges
1 lemon
1 1/4 cups (300 mL) water
1/2 cup (125 mL) sugar

Remove rind from mandarins and zest from lemon and julienne finely. Remove pith from lemon and discard. Chop the flesh of the lemon and mandarins.

In a stainless steel saucepan, bring the mandarin rind, lemon zest and water to a boil. Cover, reduce heat and simmer gently for 20 minutes. Check after 15 minutes to make sure it doesn't boil dry.

Add the lemon and mandarin flesh to saucepan and continue simmering, covered, for 20 minutes. Add the sugar, increase heat to high and boil rapidly, uncovered, until syrup forms a gel, about 10 minutes for a small batch. Remove from heat. Pour into a sterilized glass jar, seal and let cool. Refrigerate for up to 3 months.

Dried Cranberry and Candied Orange Confit

During the holiday season, have this on hand to fill mini tarts, to sandwich shortbread or sugar cookies, or to fold into whipped cream for a Cranberry Fool. It keeps for a month in the fridge, so if you make it at the end of November, you'll have it around throughout December. It's also a great hostess gift in a pretty jar tied with raffia or a wide satin ribbon.

Makes 1 1/2 cups (375 mL)

Grated zest of 1 orange, finely julienned
Juice of 2 large oranges
1 1/2 cups (375 mL) dried cranberries
1/2 cup (125 mL) liquid honey
1/2 cup (125 mL) sugar

In a saucepan of boiling water, blanch the orange zest for 1 minute; drain and set aside until using.

In a small saucepan over low heat, combine the orange juice, cranberries, honey and sugar; simmer until it reaches the consistency of syrup and is reduced to about 1 1/2 cups (375 mL). Add the orange zest and stir to combine. Transfer to a bowl and set aside to cool.

Spoon into sterilized glass jars and refrigerate until using. Confit can be refrigerated for up to 4 months.

Chocolate

Chocolate is a subject that's very dear to my heart – or should I say my waistline? When I was a child, I wasn't too thrilled by chocolate; I was always the one who ordered the strawberry milkshake or had the butter pecan ice cream cone. That was before I had been exposed to really great dark chocolate: semi-sweet or bitter-sweet Valrhona, Callebaut and Scharffen Berger, just for starters. Once I entered the culinary world and experienced real chocolate, I couldn't turn back. Now I have to work at controlling my desire to indulge too often.

Fortunately, a little good chocolate goes a long way. Try this test: buy a bar of basic chocolate, such as a Hershey's bar, and one of Scharffen Berger or Valrhona dark chocolate with a minimum of 60 per cent cocoa content. Taste a small square of the dark chocolate: it will melt in your mouth and taste slightly bitter, maybe even tart, with a long finish that will stay with you. The other chocolate bar will be sweet right away, but then go flat; before you know it, you will have eaten the whole bar and barely even noticed. There's no long finish and no real satisfaction.

Another test I often do at my cooking classes, just to see the reactions, is to have everyone sample Baker's semi-sweet chocolate and then Valrhona or Callebaut. First-timers are always astonished at the difference. It's worth the effort and additional cost to buy better chocolate. If you're going to all the trouble of making a chocolate dessert, use the best chocolate you can find and you'll be rewarded with great results.

At LSFF, we've used top-quality chocolate right from the beginning. As Callebaut chocolate is now made in Calgary, it's easy to find in most Canadian cities. It was our chocolate of choice until we tried Valrhona from France. Suddenly the bar was raised; I actually started hiding Valrhona chocolate around my house – in case of emergency only. Now I use Callebaut in most of my baking, but Valrhona stars in recipes where chocolate has the lead role. I also like Scharffen Berger chocolate from California.

Chocolate is temperature sensitive, so don't store it in the fridge. It keeps best in a dark place at 68 to 72°F (20 to 22°C). In a pinch, you can use cocoa powder in place of chocolate by mixing 1 tbsp (15 mL) melted unsalted butter with 3 tbsp (45 mL) cocoa powder.

Crispy Chocolate-Dipped Orange Slices

I love making these during the holiday season. They're delicious to serve with coffee after dessert as an extra little treat. At LSFF, we would sometimes put them in our cookie crates to add a sophisticated touch.

Makes about 3 dozen

2 cups (500 mL) sugar
1/4 cup (50 mL) light corn syrup
4 seedless oranges, thinly sliced
8 oz (250 g) bittersweet chocolate, finely chopped

In a saucepan, combine the sugar, 2 cups (500 mL) water and the corn syrup; bring to a boil. Turn off heat and add the orange slices; let stand for 1 hour. Drain syrup.

Preheat the oven to 350°F (180°C).

On a baking sheet fitted with a cooling rack, arrange orange slices in single layer. Bake for 5 minutes. Reduce temperature to 200°F (100°C) and let oranges dry in oven for 4 hours. Or turn off the oven and let dry overnight. Peel oranges off the cooling rack and set aside.

In a double boiler over simmering water, melt 6 oz (180 g) of the chocolate, stirring often with a rubber spatula, until melted. Remove from heat and blend in remaining chocolate, 1 tbsp (15 mL) at a time, allowing it to melt after each addition. This tempers, or cools, the chocolate to the proper temperature for dipping. If you want to test it with a thermometer, it should read 88 to 90°F (31 to 32°C).

Dip the orange slices in the chocolate; shake off excess and place on a waxed paper–lined baking sheet. Refrigerate until chocolate sets, about 15 minutes. Store between layers of waxed paper in an airtight container for up to 3 weeks, or in the freezer for up to 2 months.

Mulled Winter Nuts

These nuts sing of the holidays – the smell and taste are all about fond memories and tradition. Every year at Christmas, we package these by the dozens. They make a fantastic little gift for friends.

Makes 6 cups (1.5 L)

2 cups (500 mL) pecans
2 cups (500 mL) almonds
1 cup (250 mL) walnuts
1 cup (250 mL) cashews
1 egg white, lightly beaten

Spice Mix:
2 cups (500 mL) icing sugar
1/2 cup (125 mL) cornstarch
1/2 cup (125 mL) cinnamon
2 tsp (10 mL) sea salt
2 tsp (10 mL) ground ginger
1 tsp (5 mL) ground cloves
1 tsp (5 mL) ground nutmeg

Spice Mix: In a bowl, combine the icing sugar, cornstarch, cinnamon, salt, ginger, cloves and nutmeg; mix well.

In another bowl, mix together the pecans, almonds, walnuts and cashews; stir in the egg white, coating nuts as evenly as possible. Sprinkle the Spice Mix on a tray and roll the nuts in the mix to coat. Let stand for 30 minutes, stirring occasionally.

Preheat the oven to 250°F (120°C).

Line a baking sheet with parchment paper. Remove the nuts from the mix and place on the baking sheet. Sprinkle with some of the mix on the pan. Bake until the nuts are roasted and the coating is dry, about 1 hour. Remove from oven, let cool and sift excess spice mixture from nuts.

Rosemary Orange Almonds

Although we're known for our vast arrays of artful hors d'oeuvres, when I'm having a dinner party at home, I try to curb the intake of nibblies, so as not to spoil everyone's appetite. Served warm alongside some fabulous olives, these almonds will keep everyone content until dinner is served.

Makes 4 cups (1 L)

4 cups (1 L) unroasted blanched almonds
1 egg white, lightly beaten
4 tsp (20 mL) packed brown sugar
1 tsp (5 mL) sea salt
1/4 tsp (1 mL) cayenne pepper
1 tbsp (15 mL) minced fresh rosemary
1/2 tsp (2 mL) orange oil
Finely grated zest of 1 orange

Preheat the oven to 300°F (150°C).

Spread the almonds on a baking sheet and roast for 15 minutes; set aside to let cool.

Reduce the temperature to 250°F (120°C). Line a baking sheet with parchment paper.

In a bowl, combine the almonds, egg white, sugar, salt, cayenne, rosemary, orange oil and orange zest; mix thoroughly. Spread nut mixture evenly on prepared pan; roast, stirring occasionally, until crisp and dry, about 25 minutes.

Holiday Ham with Bourbon Glaze and Winter Fruit Stuffing

For the special holiday meal, LSFF uses a ham that's already cooked; it certainly makes life easier. Simply stuff the ham, baste with the glaze and bake until it's warmed through. There may be instructions for heating the ham on the wrapper, but bear in mind that with stuffing it takes longer to heat. If you're baking an 8- to 10-lb (4 to 5 kg) ham, plan on about one hour at 350°F (180°C) to heat the meat and stuffing.

Makes 18 servings

1 precooked boneless leg of ham, 8 to 10 lb (4 to 5 kg)
Winter Fruit Stuffing (recipe follows)

Bourbon Glaze:
1/2 cup (125 mL) red wine
1/2 cup (125 mL) bourbon
1/2 cup (125 mL) packed brown sugar
3 tbsp (45 mL) grainy mustard
2 tbsp (30 mL) finely grated orange peel
6 cloves

Preheat the oven to 350°F (180°C).

Bourbon Glaze: In a saucepan over medium-high heat, combine the wine, bourbon, sugar, mustard, orange peel and cloves; bring to a boil. Reduce heat and simmer until reduced by half. Remove from heat and let cool.

Slather the ham with the glaze. Bake for 1 hour, basting after 30 minutes and again 10 minutes before removing from oven.

Many of our customers are excited about the inclusion of this recipe in the book, because this stuffing became a favourite at LSFF during the holiday season. We use it to stuff whole legs of ham, but it would also be delicious in the centre of a crown roast of pork or served on the side as an accompaniment to pork roast or chops. It will keep refrigerated for two weeks. I love having it the day after the big dinner, heaped onto thin slices of leftover ham stuffed inside a crusty roll with a slather of Dijon mustard.

Winter Fruit Stuffing

Makes 4 cups (1 L), enough for 1 boneless leg of ham

1 cup (250 mL) dried apricots
1 cup (250 mL) dried figs, halved
1 cup (250 mL) dried cranberries
1 cup (250 mL) golden raisins
1 cup (250 mL) red wine
1/2 cup (125 mL) sugar
1/2 cup (125 mL) water
1 cinnamon stick

In a large heavy saucepan over medium-low heat, combine the apricots, figs, cranberries, raisins, wine, sugar, water and cinnamon stick; simmer gently until the fruit is plumped and the liquid is reduced to about 1/2 cup (125 mL), about 30 minutes. Remove cinnamon stick and discard. Let come to room temperature before stuffing ham.

Sun-Dried Cranberry and Hazelnut Stuffing

Another favourite holiday staple, this recipe actually inspired one of our most popular Raincoast Crisp flavours. It's very West Coast – we see fields of cranberries being harvested every fall, and not too far into the Fraser Valley there are miles of hazelnut orchards. If you're a fan of sausage in your stuffing, simply add 1 lb (500 g) of your favourite sausage meat, cooked, drained and crumbled, before adding the stock.

Makes 8 cups (2 L), enough for an 18- to 20-lb (9 to 10 kg) turkey

4 tbsp (60 mL) butter
1/2 large onion, diced
1 cup (250 mL) hazelnuts, toasted and coarsely chopped
1/2 cup (125 mL) sun-dried cranberries
2 tbsp (30 mL) finely chopped fresh rosemary
2 tbsp (30 mL) finely chopped fresh thyme
2 tbsp (30 mL) finely chopped fresh parsley
1 tsp (5 mL) finely chopped fresh sage
Sea salt and freshly ground pepper
1 lb (500 g) focaccia bread, cut into 1-inch (2.5 cm) cubes
3 cups (375 mL) chicken stock (approx.)

In a heavy sauté pan over medium heat, melt the butter; sauté the onions until softened. Stir in the hazelnuts, cranberries, rosemary, thyme, parsley and sage; season to taste with salt and pepper. Add the bread cubes. Pour in enough stock, 1/2 cup (125 mL) at a time, to just moisten bread.

Stuff into the cavity of the turkey before roasting. Or, if you wish to serve it as a side dish, transfer to a casserole dish and bake in 375°F (190°C) oven for 30 to 45 minutes, until the stuffing is heated through with a golden crust on top.

Christmas Trifle with Marsala

Everyone has traditions at Christmas, especially when it comes to holiday treats. This alternative to the classic English dessert has long been a favourite at LSFF. Even better is that it's best made a day or two in advance.

Makes 8 to 10 servings

1 panettone, crust removed
1 cup (250 mL) apricot preserves
Marsala
1/4 cup (50 mL) slivered almonds, toasted
1 1/2 cups (375 mL) heavy cream
1 tsp (5 mL) vanilla extract
Belgian chocolate curls (see Making Chocolate Curls, page 161)

Custard:
6 egg yolks
1/2 cup (125 mL) sugar
2 cups (500 mL) milk
1 tsp (5 mL) vanilla extract

Cut the panettone into fingers; spread each side of fingers with apricot preserves. Arrange a layer of fingers in the bottom of a large serving bowl; sprinkle with Marsala and almonds. Repeat layering.

Custard: In a bowl, beat the egg yolks with the sugar; set aside. In a saucepan, bring the milk to a boil; pour over the egg yolk mixture and mix well. Return mixture to saucepan. Reduce heat to low and cook, stirring, until the custard coats the back of the spoon. Watch carefully because it will thicken suddenly. Remove from heat and stir in the vanilla. Immediately pour the custard over the panettone in the serving bowl, puncturing the cake with a knife here and there to ensure it absorbs the custard. Let cool. Cover and refrigerate until serving.

Whip the cream with the vanilla extract; pile over the trifle. Sprinkle with chocolate curls.

Cranberry Cosmopolitan

The TV series *Sex and the City* put this drink on the map, and it continues to be a hit – particularly at Christmas, thanks to its gorgeous ruby colour and cranberry garnish. At large parties, I always try to offer a special drink like this as an alternative to the ubiquitous wine and beer.

Makes 10 drinks

1 1/4 cups (300 mL) Grand Marnier
1 1/4 cups (300 mL) cranberry juice cocktail
1 1/4 cups (300 mL) fresh lime juice
4 cups (1 L) chilled champagne or sparkling wine

Stir together Grand Marnier and cranberry and lime juices. Cover and refrigerate until chilled, about 2 hours, or for up to 6 hours. Just before serving, divide among 10 champagne flutes and top off with champagne. Serve immediately.

Lesley's Pantry

Dry Pantry

Active dry yeast
All-purpose flour
Almonds
Anchovies
Apple cider vinegar
Arrowroot
Artichoke hearts
Baking powder
Baking soda
Balsamic vinegar
Beans: cannellini, black
  beans, lentils, etc.
Brandy
Candied ginger
Capers
Chocolate, especially
  products with 60 to 70 per
  cent cocoa; I like Callebaut,
  Valrhona and Scharffen
  Berger brands
Cinnamon sticks
Cointreau
Cornmeal
Dijon mustard
Dried apples
Dried apricots
Dried cherries
Dried figs, especially
  Calimyrna and Mission

Dutch-process cocoa powder:
  I like Valrhona, Scharffen
  Berger and Bensdorp
Espresso powder
Flaked coconut
Flaxseed
Gelatin
Graham cracker crumbs
Hazelnut oil
Hazelnuts
Late-harvest Riesling
Liquid honey
Macadamia nuts
Marsala
New potatoes
Oat bran
Oatmeal
Olive oil: extra-virgin
  and regular
Olives: niçoise, Arbequina,
  Picholine, kalamata
Pasta: especially Martelli,
  Rusticella
Pearl barley
Pecans
Pine nuts
Pistachios
Prunes
Pumpkin: canned
  unsweetened purée
Pure vanilla extract

Raisins, especially Thomson
Red wine
Red wine vinegar
Sea salt: fine and coarse
Sugar: white, golden brown and
  icing (confectioner's)
Sun-dried tomatoes
Tomato ketchup
Tomatoes: canned plum,
  especially Italian brands
Rice: carnaroli and arborio for
  risotto, basmati, jasmine
Vegetable oil
Vermouth
Wheat bran
Wheat germ
White vinegar
White wine
Wild rice
Yukon Gold potatoes

If you want to make interesting variations on your old standbys without constantly running to the grocery store every time you pick up a cookbook, it's essential to have a well-stocked pantry. If you do, you can be more spontaneous and adventuresome more often. Of course, not everyone has enough cupboard, fridge and freezer space to stock everything I've listed here. So you make the call according to your preferences and cooking style. I also encourage you to seek out vendors who specialize in particular ingredients and offer better, fresher and, possibly, more local product than the big chains. Cook global, but buy local as much as possible.

Spices

Allspice

Bay leaves

Black pepper: especially
  Tellicherry and Malabar

Cayenne pepper

Celery seed

Cinnamon

Ground cumin

Nutmeg

Saffron threads

Smoked paprika

Sweet paprika

Yellow mustard seed

Refrigerator

Asiago

Cambozola

Chèvre

Feta: preferably sheep's milk

Garlic

Gingerroot

Lemons

Limes

Onions: red and white

Oranges

Parmesan cheese

Prosciutto

Shallots

Freezer

Bacon and pancetta

Basil pesto

Butter, unsalted

Chicken stock

Demi-glace

Phyllo pastry

Sun-dried tomato pesto

Won ton wrappers

Kitchen Equipment

Barbecue

Blender

Cast-iron skillet:
  8-inch (20 cm)

Citrus juicer

Colander

Cutting board: a large
  wooden one

Dutch oven: 8-quart (8 L)

Electric mixer

Food processor

Grater

Heatproof spatulas

Knives: paring knife, serrated
  bread knife, boning and carv-
  ing knife, eight-inch chef's
  knife, Santuko knife

Ladles: small, medium, large

Measuring cups

Measuring spoons

Metal spoons: slotted
  and solid

Non-stick heavy skillet:
  14-inch (35 cm)

Rasp (very fine grater)

Ricer (for potatoes)

Saucepans: 2- and 4-quart
  (2 and 4 L)

Sauté pans: 7-inch (18 cm) and
  10-inch (25 cm)

Scale

Sieve

Stainless steel mixing bowls

Stockpot: 8-quart (8 L)

Vegetable peeler

Whisks

Wooden spoons

Acknowledgements

Along the way, many people helped to create this book. I'd like to thank everyone who contributed.

I can't thank Jill Lambert enough for her role in making this book happen. It definitely would not have come together without her. Jill's expertise in spearheading this project made her a pleasure to work with. Her tireless attention to detail, organization and enthusiasm were crucial to the success of this book. Thank you so much, Jill.

I asked a group of friends, all accomplished amateur cooks, to test the recipes in their home kitchens and let me know how they turned out. Their comments helped to refine the recipes and ensured the best results. My thanks to:

Maggie Aro, Karen Bruk, Sarah Catliff, Ann Gibbs, Carol Jukes, Niki Garnett, Wendy Hamilton, Leslie Hoeschen, Alison Lambert, Kelley Lindahl, Ginny Love, Beth Noble, Elaine Stearman, Elaine Stevens, Virginia Richards, Lynne Rose and Linda Yorke.

These recipes were collected over years of catering; not all of them were in tidy electronic formats. My thanks to Harry Young for inputting the recipes and creating a clean, organized manuscript.

My working recipes don't always display both imperial and metric measurements. Thanks to Brenda Thompson for doing the conversions.

Julia Armstrong did a great job of copy-editing this manuscript. She made the manuscript much cleaner and more consistent. Shaun Oakey proofread the pages and helped to smooth out any rough edges. Thanks to them both.

Profound thanks to the people at HarperCollins: Kirsten Hanson, Iris Tupholme, Noelle Zitzer, Felicia Quon, Neil Erickson and designer Alan Jones. It's been a pleasure to work with you.

Thanks to Yvonne Duivenvoorden and Neil Barnett for the photos, Claire Stubbs for the food styling and Catherine Doherty for the photo props.

To all the customers of LSFF, I would like to thank you for your support, encouragement and inspiration. Thanks to:

Hiroko Ainsworth, Kathy Armstrong, Claudia Beck, Irene Calder, Doris Bradstreet Daughney, George Deagan, Bette and Max Dutch, Barbara Gillanders, Andrew Graham, Carol Henriquez, Cathy Howden, Barb Kemp, Grace MacDonald, Timmy Mackay-Dunn, Debbie Mckeen, Stephanie Nicolls, Diane Norton, Lee-Ann Panther, Suzanne Price, Nicky Seppala, Janet Scott, Michael Scott, Sarah Scott, Cate Simpson, Craig Stowe, David Stowe, Elisabet Stowe, Mary-Anne Stowe, Marianne Thomson, Tina Tier, Mary Wesik, Gail West, Karen Westlake, Jenny Whittall, Maybo Wu and all the people who have worked at Lesley Stowe Fine Foods over the past 20 years, who are too numerous to mention but have all contributed to making this book happen.

Index

Z

Zabaglione, 163